The Mask They Wear

Written by
H. Paul Cote

For Resale information or to ask about other Books Please Contact Paul Cote at
3348 Arkansas Rd. West Monroe La. 71291
Paulcotes@yahoo.com

Chapter

Introduction

Inspired by true stories; It's about a close-knit team with the top 10 people in the world, that are Human trafficking Lords, that's in a market today spread around the globe from the top to bottom, they buy, sale, and trade, teenage girls as if they were used cars, they sold to brothels, the general house slave girl, a concubine, prostitution, or for body parts, your friend or a family member may get one of their kidneys. Going once, going twice, sold to the highest bidder, for $25.000. This is an action-packed thriller with some horror scenes.

This is an action-packed thriller with some strong scenes. Warning comes with strong language. Designed for the young adult readers.

Disclosure Warning

The literature in this book was more Design for the 21 or above reader, not designed for young readers under the age of 18, the stories can be very submissive, with strong language, and mental imaging, so please be advised this is not permitted for young readers under the age of 18 years of age.

This is intended for an adult audience only, if you're not of legal age leave now and come back when you are of legal age.

If you are of legal age but listening to informative sexual contents in the privacy of your own home and is not permitted in your community you should not listen to this audio-book but you immediately should move to a more open minded community.

This is a fine collection of stories of pleasure to enjoy upon hours of reading, and to reread at a later date, please don't exercise the stories.

Chapter 1

Dr. Novak looks out the port window as his plane lands at the Miami airport. He can tell it's a misty morning and can hear the tires screech against the runway. He can't wait to depart from the plane.

As he steps off into the enclosed walkway he can feel the fall coolness against his skin coming in from the opening. He glances at his watch, the excitement is eating at him, "I only have an couple of hours till I meet up with the real estate agent, to see my new beach house." The man was grinning from ear to ear, barely able to contain himself.

He walks through the large, double doors of the airport and notices a lounge to his left. "Why not kill some time with a couple of drinks?"

Entering the lounge, he looks around and notices a young couple sitting at the table in the corner, kissing and fondling one another. "Lucky dog. I'd like to join them." Excitement builds inside him as he stares at them. He takes a seat at the bar where he can continue to watch them, hiding his oncoming erection.

Breaking his attention from the couple for a moment, he looks around for the bartender. He was nowhere to be found. "Maybe they are in the back." So he returns his attention to the couple and watches as the man's hand goes under the table and under the woman's skirt.

Lost in his own excitement, he doesn't hear the bartender approach, "What can I get for you?" she asked.

"Red headed slut in a cup." He replies coolly as he turns around in the stool, trying his best to appear smooth.

She cocks her eyebrow, "I've never heard of it, but if you tell me what's in it I will whip it up for you."

"Oh, it's pretty simple, you just take some peach snaps, add a little bit of Jaeger Meister and cranberry juice (the dark red is the best) and a little bit of ice. Then you shake it and there you have it." Novak leans forward over the bar, holding his chin up with one hand as he gives the girl a flirty smirk. "Now, do I get a discount for telling you that secret?"

She knew he was hitting on her and she figured he probably just made that drink up himself. But just as every female bartender must do she kept her cool and just made what he asked for. "Well now... I guess you learn something new every day, don't ya?" as she mixed his drink together.

"Yes, I guess we do. Where is your accent from? I love it."

"Louisiana!" she stated, proudly. "What about you? Where did you fly in from?"

"Los Angeles. I'm taking over a dental practice." He couldn't help but mentally undress her as he spoke.

"Oh, so you're a dentist? How interesting. I need a dentist. I have a loose cap."

"I will take care of that when I get my practice set up." He takes a few sips of his drink while digging around in his wallet and drops what he owed her onto the bar. He glanced at his watch, "I have to go. Can you tell me how to get over to North Miami Avenue? Oh and, the best place to rent a car around here?"

"You can rent a car at Metro Auto Agency, right across the street from the main entrance of the airport."

"...and how do I get to Ocean Dr., Miami Beach?"

"I don't really know. They probably can tell you at the rental car office. Is that where you're going to be staying?"

Dr Novak looks down at his watch, "I have got to go." He exits out the main entrance of the airport and locates the auto agency that she was talking about. He notices a charcoal grey Porsche in the rent-a-car lot, "That's the one I want."

Entering the car-agency office, he notices an agent. A beautiful, well dressed woman with long slender legs, and a tantalizing expression on her face. He was instantly mesmerized. "What can I do for you?" she asked.

Glancing at her figure again he thinks, "If you only knew." Then he says to the woman, "I need to rent a car... and I want that grey Porsche out front."

"We can set that up for you. Just a little paper work and I'll have you on your way."

As he signs the final paper he asks "What is the easiest route to Ocean Drive, Miami Beach?"

She smiles at him and says, "There's a GPS built into the dash. Just enter your address and you're on the way. Is there anything else I can help you with?" As she says that he looks her over one last time, focusing attention on her hot, pouty lips. Then his eyes wander down to her full, perky breasts.

When she directs him to find the car, he turns and exits, gets in the car, enters the address into the GPS and drives off.

After several miles, he makes his way to Ocean Drive. He looks at his piece of paper with the address. "He's in the 2000 block. 2015." He looks back up and notices 2011... 2013... 2015.

There's a white van in the driveway with some kind of sign on the door. "I hope that is the agent and hope it's not rented already. He pulls into the driveway and gets out. Looking at the white van again, he sees the real-estate company logo on the door. He is relieved. "I hope it's still available, I would hate to find out it's already taken.

Walking on down to the house he looks around and notices all the tall, slender palm trees. They remind him of skinny legs on a woman in a tight bikini. Beautiful blue sky, pink outlining the foreground. But what really grabs his eye are the two girls, walking down the sidewalk in tight slender bikinis. He flashes them a smile, only one waves back to him.

He walks to the door and rings the bell. The real-estate agent opens the door "Hello, you must be Dr. Novak." She said.

"Yes. You must be Connie."

"Yes, Sir, that's right. It's nice to finally meet you in person. Come this way and we will get started on the tour. Let me show you the main interest first."

"That would be the bedroom." He says flirtatiously.

"Sure, right this way." He follows behind her, undressing her with his eyes, wondering how she is in bed. Visualizing her on top of him with sweat glittering on her naked body. He has a desire to hear her say his name.

As they walk into the bedroom he sees the ocean through a huge glass window. He walks through the sliding glass doors and onto the deck. From up there he can see the huge dock, protruding out into the water. "Perfect for my plans," He turns to Connie "I'll take it."

Laying the papers out atop a patio table she gives him a smile. "Wonderful. I have the paperwork right here. All you have to do is sign here and here."

She hands him a pen and as he signs the paperwork, "Connie can you tell me how to get to North Miami Avenue? I have another appointment to look at. An office space."

"North Miami Avenue? Hmm… Go back out the way you came and get on Highway 195. Take the Julia Tuttle Causeway back to the inland. Then turn on 95 north and go a little ways til you see the exit for North Miami Ave. Just that easy. Anything else I can help you with?" Then remembering, "Oh by the way, here're the keys for the front and the back doors. I hope you really enjoy your new house. It's one of the nicest ones in this area.

Doctor Novak gives Connie a cute little hug from excitement, adding a little kiss up under her ear. He walks her out to her Van, telling her about his practice.

He walks around to get in his car, but he couldn't help to notice how cute she is. He will have to come up with an excuse to call her, to go out for dinner. Or a late night supper. He types the address into the GPS, the car almost drove itself down there. He first turned on North Miami Avenue. He looked down at his notes. He's looking for the Shamrock tower office building. "Continue down the avenue a little ways…" He keeps notes of all the cute girls walking. He is already making plans in his mind and is very excited about being able to execute his plan.

He turns his head back around and notices a sign, "Shamrock Towers Parking Garage"

"This parking garage could really come in handy for privacy." He turns on his left blinker and eases into the parking area. He stops as he starts to come up on a guard post.

He pulls up. The guard steps out to his car. "Who you here to see?"

Lifting his head and looking straight at the rent-a-cop, "I'm Doctor Novak. I have an appointment here this morning, to look at some office space up on the third floor."

"Yes. Just go ahead straight, until you see an overhead sign that has parking garage on it, and keep going. It will loop around to the second level and continue on around to the third level. There will be a door going into the hallway. You will find the receptionist up there that can give you guidance."

Doctor Novak gave the guard a pleasing smile, nodded and drove off; following the drive up to the third level. He quickly finds an empty space and parks his vehicle, keeping a quick pace to make sure he's not late for this deal. He notices the door going into the building and heads down the hallway until he sees the receptionist's counter on the right. As he makes his way to the counter he notices she is really a cutie-pie with her cute little dimples and short, curly red hair.

She smiles, "Can I help you?"

Thinking to himself while looking at her, "If I ever got you in my dentist chair you would be fucked. I need to come back later and make an excuse to get to know her."

"Yes, I am Doctor Novak and I'm looking for suite 312. Can you tell me how to find it?"

"Sure. Go down this hallway and make a right. It's at the end. You will see it on the left. Are you the new dentist who's going to be replacing Doctor Sullivan?

"Yes I am. You're such a good guesser. I tell you what... for good guessers I always offer a special. When you get ready to get your teeth cleaned, you come see me. I will make you a special deal since you have been so helpful. I've got to go. I'm running late. Come down and set the appointment when you get ready."

Chapter 2

Dr. Novak begins making his way down the hall. It stays on his mind, "What I'd like to do with her." He turns the corner and sees Suite 312, exposing itself on the sign protruding out from the wall. Turning the door knob to the waiting room he enters. Feeling a sense of ownership he whispers, "Everything is going be okay."

He walks over to the receptionist's window and taps on it lightly. "I'm Doctor Novak. I'm here getting my teeth cleaned.

The little receptionist girl begins shuffling, looking for her appointment book and thumbing through today's appointments, "I don't see your name. What was it again?"

"Doctor Novak."

She looks up with a giggly grin, "I know who you are. We had been expecting you today. Doctor Sullivan is in the back. Go through this door and follow me to his office."

"Tap tap. Knock knock."

Doctor Sullivan shouted, "Come in,"

The receptionist turns the knob and pushes the door open, "This is Doctor Novak. I've got to go back up front. It is good to have you with us, Doctor Novak."

The receptionist turns and reaches around to close the door of the office. Dr. Novak turns his head to say, "Thank you," but mainly to give him a chance to look at her ass wiggle as she walks away. One leg looks like it comes up, arched over to the other one, "What a beautiful shape. I hope to get some of that, eventually."

"Doctor Novak," Doctor Sullivan replies, "I hope you had a pleasant trip. Are you ready to take over the practice? I have all the paperwork right here, from my lawyer. If you'd like to take a moment to look them over, that would be fine. And if you see anything we need to discuss, bring it to my attention. But if everything looks satisfactory, then just sign on the dotted line. We will have our business completed, with the amount of money we discussed on the phone.

Doctor Novak takes a moment to glance over the bill of sale. Then he looks up, "It looks real good. And yes, the price is the same as we discussed. ... and I see you're leaving me all the furnishings, including dental chairs, supplies, and tools ...everything that goes with the business?" Dr. Novak reaches over and picks up the pen that was laying on the table, and slides his hand down to the bottom of the page. Signed and dated, he hands it back to Doctor Sullivan.

"Where are you planning to go for your retirement, Doctor Sullivan?"

"Texas. Most of my family lives in Texas. Tomorrow I become a cowboy. Ye high! Ride dumb little doggie." The older doctor laughs at himself. "I will be a cowboy from that day forward. Well Doctor Novak, I've already got my personal things packed up and I'm ready to head out the door." Stretching out his hand, "Good luck with your practice. If you have any questions, just give me a call. Here's my number."

Doctor Sullivan exits out the door. Dr. Novak makes his way back to the receptionist's desk, this time, on the inside of the counter. The first thing he notices are her grapefruit-sized hooters, then her slender legs, how one wrapped over the top of the other one like the golden arches of McDonald's. He stays quiet a little longer to look at her. "She does look cute. I'm tempted to make it a rule that she has to wear shorter dresses."

Dr. Novak says, "We were not introduced. What is your name?"

The girl whips around in her swivel chair, startled by presence. "My name is Patty, Doctor Novak. Would you like me to reschedule any of your appointments? Or continue as planned for today. You have one coming up in an hour. Then we have walk-ins from time to time."

"Let's leave it like it is. I'll go ahead and see the next. I believe I'll just roam around the office and the examination room, getting familiar with where things are. Just let me know when the next one's here."

Patty sits there, waiting for the next appointment to walk in. She hears the door open from the hallway. A very young, cute, petite girl walks in, "Yes ma'am. My name is Kathy, and I called the other day to set up an appointment with the dentist."

"Yes. I see your name. Please, have a seat in the waiting room. I'll tell the dentist you're here."

Kathy sits there, her teeth were throbbing, "It's taking forever." She turns to look at the receptionist. "My girlfriend told me about him. He has helped a lot of people she knows, since he opened in our area down on the south side. She also said that he's from Las Vegas where he had a dental practice. I wonder why he moved here. Las Vegas is a lot nicer than this place. If it would've been me, I would had stayed there and surely make more money, than being here. Well anyhow, I hope he's reasonable or can work out something with me. I have GOT to get something done with these teeth. The pain is more than I can bear at times.

Patty slides open the receptionist window and motions with her finger, for the girl come over. When she makes her way over to the window, Patty tells her, "We are starting with a new doctor today. The other one has gone into retirement. This doctor's name is Doctor Novak and I'm sure he'll be glad to see you. Can I get your name again, so I can add to the appointment book?"

"My name is Kathy. My teeth are hurting really bad."

"Kathy, you can go back, now. The dentists will see you. Go into examination room "B" and sit in the chair. Wait for the dentist. He'll be in there soon.

Kathy sits there and begins to get a little nervous, thinking about everything. Not only about having her mouth worked on, but also the money. She didn't hardly have any money. "... and my mom threw me out four or five months ago. It's been hard on me, living on the streets, doing whatever it takes to survive. I pick up a little money here and a little money there, doing odd jobs, but it is hardly enough to pay for my motel room; which I am glad they rent by the week." Kathy's roommate is an old high school friend of hers. She works at an Italian restaurant, within walking distance. She's always brings home food that's going to the dumpster. So, a little here and little there, they managed to scrape by, which is better than some they know.

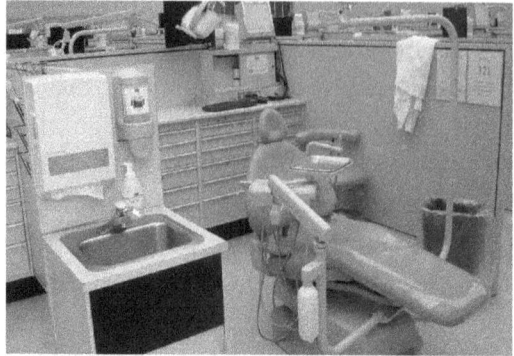

The door opens and a man in a lab coat walks on in.

"Are you Kathy? I am Doctor Novak. I understand you're having trouble with your teeth. Why don't you go ahead and lay back in the chair and open your mouth. I'll see what you got in there" Then there is a long pause. "Hum! Okay, Kathy. You can rest your mouth now. It doesn't look good. You're going to need a good deal of work done. On the top, you will need the three broken teeth pulled, and replace them with a partial plate. I think I can match your original teeth. But on the bottom, three of your teeth can be capped.

"Kathy. Do you have insurance, with your work? Or an independent insurance plan? This could really add up."

Shrugging her shoulders, "I don't have any insurance." She looks up at him with a concerned look on her face. "...but I do have some money put back. If I could bring you that and see if we can work out the balance? I really do need to get something done. They are constantly hurting." Dr. Novak stands back to look at Kathy.

"It feels like he is checking me out, or maybe he is just concerned."

"Go back out into the waiting room and talk to the receptionist. Give her all your information so she can set you up an appointment to come back. We'll go from there or at least get started. We'll talk about what we can do to work something out."

She walks out of his office. Doctor Novak begins to have erotic thoughts. How he is going to help her to work out her dental bill? Or should I say, how I'm going to work out Kathy's dentist bill, for Kathy is an exceptionally beautiful girl, even her body is the type Doctor Novak is attracted to. "She has average, long, slender legs. Not fat, but firm and full. An hourglass shaped body that protruded into two very nice breasts, the size of grapefruits. They were attached to very slim arms. Her face has very attractive features, like her nose that turns up on the end. Her ears are small and cute. As far as the good doctor goes. She would make good candidates for sale, if I can get a hold of Jonathan in Los Angeles to see if he has someone to come pick her up."

"Buzz, buzz, buzz," Dr Novak feels his phone vibrating in his pocket. He goes to pull it out. It's Jonathan, calling him from Los Angeles.

"Hello. This is Novak... I was just fixing the call you. Do you have a sweet tooth? I have a banana top with blueberries, here."

These are codes we use in the underground. It gives information to the trafficking agent. He is the one that comes and picks up the girl, and transports her back to the seaplane. From there, she will be taken to auction in one of the several nearby countries.

Jonathan said, "Yes. I got a sweet tooth. Maybe after supper."

Novak said, "I'll have it ready for you."

Doctor Novak told him that he has a blond-headed, blue-eyed girl ready for to pick up.

Jonathan was relating that he will be there in two days. Have her ready.

Chapter 3

Two days later, Kathy shows up for her appointment, in a lot of pain, "I hope the doctor will do something, today. I am beginning to have suicide tendencies. My life and my health is going down the drain. I don't know if I can take much more. My life is on the fritz." She sits over in the corner of the waiting room holding an ice pack to her throbbing jaw.

Then reception says, "Kathy. You can go back to examination room 'C'. Wait for the doctor."

As Kathy waits for him, she is in tears as the pain continues on. But Novak is actually making his way over to the receptionist first. "Hey there, sweetie," he starts with that practiced smile on his lips. "Look, I have something that I need to get done today, but there's going to be no way I can with that girl over there in C. Do you think you could do me a favor and head out to a pet store to pick my dog up some food?" He was lying, the whole thing. He didn't have a dog, but of course she didn't know that.

Patty lets out a little sigh, her eyes darting around the paperwork laid out on her desk and computer screen. "What about the office, Dr.?"

"What about it? We don't have any more patients coming in, I can handle any walk-ins myself. Can ya do it?"

She bites her lip and is about to say no, but the story about a puppy that might be starving got her. She gives a light little smile and nods. "Okay, Dr., but only cause I can't stand to see an animal go hungry."

Grinning back, Novak pats her on the shoulder. "Thanks, I'll make sure to let Oscar know who fed him tonight." He watches her leave, the fake smile he had been wearing left with her. Walking over, he locks the door behind her, not wanting to be disturbed.

Over in the examination room Kathy is laid out on the dental chair, still holding that ice pack to her jaw. As Novak walks in her eyes brighten just a little in the hope he can help her today.

"Hi, Doc, glad you could make it." She tries to joke a bit, but her mouth hurts so much that it makes her tone a bit off.

Novak gives her a smile, but it's not the joke that has him grinning. "Kathy. Try not to cry. I'm going to take care of it. Starting today, and I'll do something about the pain. I need you to lean back in the chair. Try to think about something pleasant." After a brief moment of looking at the x-rays he turns his head, looks and says, "I'm going to need to do a root canal. These can be very painful so I'm gonna put you under. Don't worry. It's just a mild sedative that will put you into a deep sleep. "

As she lay there, looking up at the ceiling, the doctor walks over behind her and opens up the cabinet. He reaches in and grabs a bottle of chloroform, puts on his rubber gloves and grabs a cloth from out of the drawer. Then he pours a medium-size wet area onto the cloth.

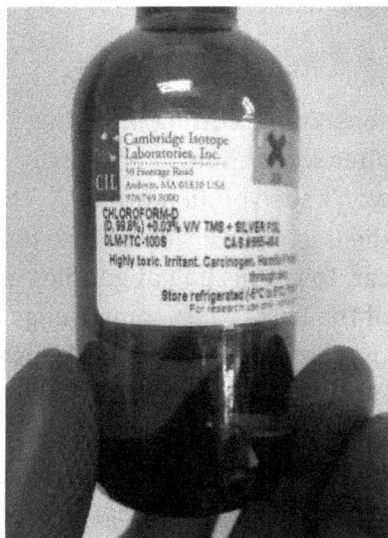

Standing behind her he reaches around, very gently he holds her head with one hand very steady. He takes his other hand, with the chloroform, and eases it over her nose. He held it there until he began to feel her body go limp. "Now Kathy Griffin. You are in my world. I have full control of you at this point. You belong to me. You're my girl." He couldn't help the sick grin that was from ear to ear on his lips as he said that. "Now, it's time to look at things in its true fashion. As it should be." Dr. Novak gets to thinking, "I dreamed about you last night. I had such erotic thoughts of ecstasy, and what I want to do to you today. I was overcome. I could not hardly sleep. Masturbating didn't even help. I just could not keep you out of my mind. But I knew I would overcome all that today. I will satisfy all my deep, strong, exotic tendencies."

Then the doctor got concerned about the receptionist. Maybe she will get back a little too early. He decides to buy himself a little more time. He calls her from his cell phone and asks her if she would mind making a couple of extra stops for him.

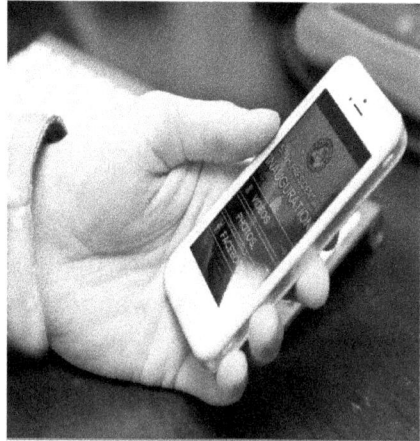

"They may be time consuming, cutting into your after work hours. I probably won't see you til morning." Then the doctor eases down into his car, to get his bag of goodies out of the trunk. Just some things that he brought from his house. It was full of his toys and play pretties. All that he needed to make this a fulfilling afternoon of pleasure for him. As he eagerly heads back up the stairs to his office, he steps inside and locks the door behind him, excitement and his erection flaring.

He knows he doesn't have any other appointments set up for this afternoon. He scampers down the hallway, standing just outside the doorway. He opens the door to examination room C and joyfully looks at her. She is laying there, limp and available, in total submission for him. He begins to undress her, starting with her little, white, tenny shoes with the bright green laces and her little pink polka-dot half socks. Then her black slacks with an office style suit. Now her little, lacy, red-pinstripe, lightly see-through, pink lace, G-string panties. "She's beginning to look like a Valentine's card, with all the colors she has on. The black pants are an envelope, and her panties and body are like the card." He gives a light chuckle then begins to sing to himself, humming a tune, "Happy Valentine's, to me. Happy Valentine's, to me. Happy Valentines, tooo mee-ee. Happy Valentines, to me." He turns around and excitedly steps over to his little bag of tricks with toys and party favors. He bends over and reaches down into his big, black bag.

"Uh-huh! This is what I have decided on?" grabbing a pair of tight rubber shorts, and a tight rubber muscle shirt, loaded down with little black sequence. He slides into his black rubber suit. "What is in my bag that I would like to dress Kathy in? How can she best pleasure me, leaving me some good memories?" He looks and pushes things around with his fingers, "Ah-ha? This looks like it would be fine if I had enough time... Woo! Now this I really like. It would look good on her. Hmm, yes. think I'm going to put this on her. Ah these are more like my colors."

After he gets dressed he picks up his big black leather bag. You know, like the old doctors had back in the mid-1800s. Then he eagerly walks back into the room, where his damsel-in-distress lay, waiting for his arrival. As she begins to move around he goes over to the counter and grabs his cloth of chloroform and eases it back over her nose, putting her back under again. Then he walks back around to her feet, saying to himself, "Ooooh, I am so going to enjoy you, girl!"

"I need to get you dressed up for me. I know you're desperately hungry for me. You want to pleasure me." She lay there, helpless. Only his burning desire in the room. He grabs his black bag of surprises. First, he pulls out a pair of pink fluffy bloomers, with rows upon rows of pink lace, and the crotch cut out of them. You know. For easy access. Then he lifts her feet and starts easing them up onto her legs, grabbing and pulling them up to her waist. Then, turning back around, he reaches down into his bag of fantasy and grabs a pink teddy top, with white flowery lace going completely around the outside and little lacy ribbons in the front, and a nice see-through back. "This corresponds very nice with the color of the bloomers."

He reaches over her and pulls her toward him. She is still plenty limp. He slides the top down onto her, bow-tying each little pink lace in the front. Excitement builds up inside him, his heart races. He reaches under the cabinet grabs the chrome stirrups, then attaches them to the chair. He reaches down, picks up her feet and slides them into the stirrups. "How cute, her polished toenails." They seem to glitter in the light. Her big toenails have a smiley face. "Mmm, Kathy, you look so beautiful, my girl."

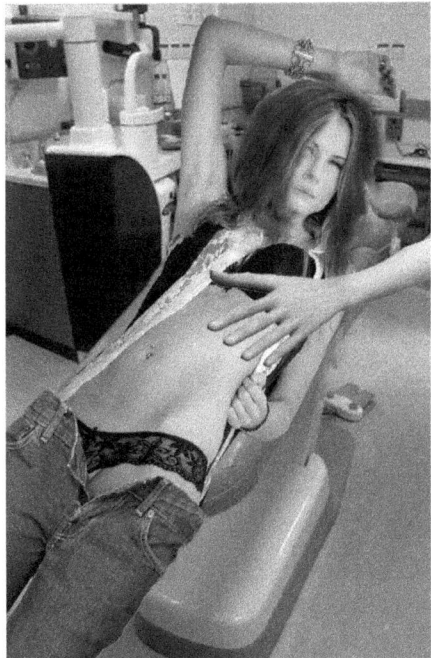

The doctor begins to get a large erection protruding through the hole cut in the front of his rubber shorts. He nestles himself in between her legs. Then adds a very small amount of slick cherry flavored jelly on to the head of his dick and eases up on her crotch. With confidence and joy he reaches down and grabs his erect penis, up close to his balls and starts rotating it round her clit. Then he slides it up and down, in between her pussy lips while looking down at the top of her vagina.

Her vaginal lips appear to be larger than most that he has seen. As he begins to stroke his dick over them, they felt very tight and firm. He wants to caress her hairless pussy with his tongue. Bending down he slowly licks it, as if he was a dog lapping water. She begins to moan and he fears she might be coming out of the deep, deep, sleep. He reaches over to his dentist tray and places the chloroform cloth back over her nose, for a second longer. He wants her somewhat responsive. Not to totally immobilize her. Just enough to paralyze her.

After a moment, he lifts the cloth back off of her nose, "I need to ease my dick up into her cunt." Running a hand up to let his fingers play on her lips lightly he smiles at her. "Kathy, sweetie, are you ready to have me inside you?" Tracing a nail along her plump lower lip his smile takes on a deranged demeanor. "Mmm, that's my girl, I knew you were."

He puts a little more cherry flavored jelly on the head of his prick and forces it up to her crotch, shoving around, looking for her hole. Once it slides in, he moans as he pushes very hard and stern. "Oh yes, you're so tight, sweetie!" He goes all the way in, trying to hit bottom. As he strokes it, back and forth, it becomes very dry. "I'm enjoying looking straight down at my dick in your pussy. Watching it go in and coming out. Going in and coming out. Your inside pussy walls stretching from my dick," Then he looks again, noticing the skin just below her lips, "Those lips would ride out on my dick."

He slides off to pull out of her. "That pussy is trying to hang on for more pleasure than I have given you." He laughs and pets her crotch lightly. "You're so eager to please me, aren't you?" He begins to pull it most all the way out, then starts to cum, but jams it back into her with strong force, quickly feeling her warm pussy tightening around his large, extended cock. He pulls it out once again and forcefully shoves it to the bottom of that cunt. Standing there, feeling a sense of relief, he continues to ejaculate, until losing all the juices out under his shaft. Then backing his shaft up, until just the head of his dick is buried in her wet womb. He reaches down with his hand and strokes his shaft back and forth at high speed, like I was masturbating. After a brief moment, he pulls completely out, leaving her to drip, creating a puddle on the floor. Exhausted, he walks over to sit down on his doctor stool. Kathy begins to move around and squirm.

The good dentist rolls his stool around to the tray holding the chloroform cloth. Once again, he places it over her nose. He was beginning to get weary from all the excitement, fun and games.

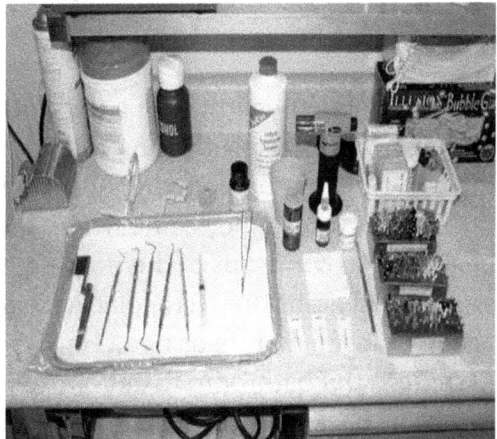

Knowing he needs to also get some work done this afternoon, he slides his tight sexy little black rubber outfit that looks like a man-sized condom suit, and drops it into the big black bag. Eagerly, he walks over and looks under the cabinet, grabbing a small metal spit bowl, a turkey baster, large napkins, a spray-bottle of disinfectant, and a small bottle of douche, hidden back behind some old books. Sitting back down on the stool and rolling himself around, he eases his way back up between her legs, takes the bottle of douche and pours it into the small spit bowl, picking up the baster.

He sucks the douche up into the baster and slides the pan directly under her womb. Then he adds some jelly to the opening and eases the baster slightly up into her. Then, with a hard fast squeeze, he sends douche all the way down to her uterus, flushing out his cum into the bowl. He removes the baster and the douche continues to slowly drip into the bowl that he placed on the floor in front of him. He reaches around, grabbing the disinfectant spray and sprays the outside of her crotch and the front side of her butt cheeks.

Wiping them off with a dry cloth, he rolls himself back, placing her feet firmly back on the floor. Then he quickly removes the two stirrups and puts them back behind the old books under the cabinet where they came from. "I've got to dress her." She is beginning to come out of the doze he put her in. He rapidly reaches around and grabs the cloth, placing it gently back on her nose, once again for just a minute or two. He lays it back on to the tray then eases into the bathroom to get himself cleaned up and dressed. As he enters back into the examination room, he decides to take one more look at her beauty. As she just lay there, she is his masterpiece.

He picks her clothes up off the floor, taking her sweater up and easing it back over her head, running her arms into the sleeves. He looks around trying to locate her black slacks. Gathering them up he starts to slide them up her legs. "The tricky part is getting them to hug her cute ass." He gets up close to her crotch. He reaches over and grabs her under her arms. He pulls her toward him, reaching down to grab her pants and pulling them up, laying her back into the chair. Zipping and fastening. He looks around for the two socks, but can only find one, "How will I explain this to her. Or should I just get rid of the one and make her think she didn't have on any socks." But as he continues to look, he finds it up under the edge of the counter. He eased the pink polka dotted socks back on her feet, located her shoes, and easily slipped them on one on the time, muttering to himself, "Damn. I'm glad it's done."

He decides not to extract the upper teeth, but to add caps to them. He reaches over and grabs the cloth, realizing it is no longer wet with chloroform. He takes the bottle of chloroform and pours another medium-size wet spot onto the cloth, placing it back over her nose. He pauses for just a moment. He picks it up, then lays it back over to the side. He grabs the tray that holds all his dental tools and perches them near his chair, looking in the box for some teeth caps that would be the same shade as her teeth.

Reaching down and opening her mouth, he takes a brief moment and sees that the three front teeth appear to be the worse and commits to placing caps on her upper three teeth.

Chapter 4

Novak starts trying to wake Kathy up. "Kathy? Kathy?" She begins to come out of the sleep. The good doctor gives her a warm and friendly smile as he holds out a bottle of medicine to her. "Kathy I have something here for you, for pain. I ran out of time this evening, but I did add caps to your upper three teeth. Take these pills for the pain. Read the instructions on the bottle. Call my office tomorrow to set up a new appointment, so we can do some more work, okay!"

Kathy nods slowly, still feeling groggy. "Uh...um yeah, okay, Doc." He walks her out through the lobby and into the hallway. Kathy turns and says, "So I need to call the office tomorrow, right?"

The good doctor Novak replies, "Yes Kathy. Just call tomorrow and set up another appointment, and don't forget to take those pills for pain."

Novak's lips curl into a half smile as he gets a peek out a window. "Oh dear, it looks like it may rain outside. You know, I'm fixing to leave here myself. If you're walking I surely wouldn't mind giving you a ride."

Holding a hand up to her head Kathy nods. "That would be nice. I don't feel like walking. I feel groggy. Yeah, thank you for a ride."

"Come back inside and sit in the waiting room." Dr. Novak places his hand under her arm to steady her, to help her sit down. "I'll get some of my things ready and then we will go." He goes off to the back and grabs a zip lock bag. Then looks for the bottle of chloroform, saturates a rag, folds it and slides it into the zip lock bag.

He stands there, "How am I going to do this?" Then it comes to him as his brain finally kicks into gear. He unbuttons the lower part of his shirt and slides the bag up inside.

He takes his jacket and lays it across his arm and walk back out into the waiting room. She is already dozing off. He walks to her, "Kathy? Kathy? You ready to go?" Then he slides his hand under her arm to help her up. They walk out into the hallway, closing the door behind, and begin the long, slow journey around to the parking garage. Although she kept stumbling over her feet, we made it to my car.

Dr. Novak helps Kathy into the passenger seat faster than a monkey grabbing a banana. He reaches in his shirt, opens up the bag, pulls out the rag, and places it over her face from behind her. When her head droops back on to the car seat he pulls the rag off, stuffing it back in the bag. "There we are sweetie, now you can just sleep all the way back home."

He finally makes it to his house. He reaches in his glove box and pulls out the garage door opener. The door contracts all the way up. He pulls into the carport, then lowers the door. "Now I feel safe," he whispers as he starts to get out.

He opens up the passenger car door and taps on her face, "Wake up. Wake up, Kathy. Let's go inside." She murmurs a bit, her eyes fluttering as she's woken and goes to nod. Dr. Novak can see he will have to help her all way inside.

"Where are we at?" she mumbles lightly, her eyes still not focusing.

"We're at my house. I wanted to show you where I live. I may get you to clean my house some time to make extra money, is that okay?"

He holds her up to keep her from falling. He unlocks the door, then carefully pushes the door open, turning the alarm off. Then he walks across the living room and down the hallway. Just under the staircase is another door, leading down into the small storm basement. He reaches around and turns the light on. They head on down and she begins to ask more questions. He reaches in his shirt to grab the magic, shut-the-fuck-up rag and places it on her face, again. He puts his arms around her body and drags her to his large oak bondage bed on the far side of the room, with chain links riveted into the side of it, as to secure rope.

He pulls her up onto to the center of the bed and begins strapping her arms to the front corner post. He sticks a black ball gag on her and ties a rag around her eyes. Then he goes down to her ankles. He grabs a long board and ties her ankles to each side, then grabbing the rope in the middle which is attached to a pulley, he begins pulling the rope until her legs are completely elevated in the air.

Kathy started coming back to her senses. She lays there for an eternity as her legs begin to go numb. "How did this happen to me? The dentist must have given me something. Must be something to do with that rag. That's it. That rag. I think he's been having sex with me. I'm real sore down there."

Kathy can hear Novak and some unfamiliar voices "Here's your money, why are you giving me that look? Didn't y'all agree on $5,000? If not, tell me so. Yes, it was $5,000. Go ahead and get her I've got to get back to work. You don't think I lay around here and fuck all day. I have to keep my hand up in somebody's dirty mouth. You, get the girl and go."

Kathy can feel her body being untied, lifted up and carried. She's so scared that she can't even move, she doesn't dare even make a sound. After a few minutes she hears the ocean waves. "We must be headed to a boat." She is still failing and woozy from whatever the dentist gave her. She feels them lifting her up and laying her on something solid.

"Let's go get the plane cranked. Let's go. The boss said for us to meet him in Mexico City right away. He said they'll have the auction in the morning." Kathy lays there for what seems like forever. She begins to feel a hand rubbing her crotch, eliciting a muffled whimper from her.

Then a voice says, "Leave her alone. The boss said she must be clean."

"I'm not going to fuck her, but I am going to eat her pussy. She's a young one. I bet she tastes good. Let me see if I can make her wet."

"Hey, she's not your bitch, dumb ass!" Kathy hears the guy that's talking walk over, his feet loud on what sound like wooden planks.

The hand at her lower region comes up and she sighs in relief. "All right, all right, jeez, man; just trying to have some fucking fun. Damn!"

And then it all breaks down for Kathy. She starts to scream as loud as she can, but all that gets by the ball in her mouth is tiny, muffled noises. One of the men laughs as he hears her. "Awww, the poor cunt is trying to holler for help. Go ahead, slut, holler all you want. No one is going to hear a thing."

Under the blindfold she starts to cry, tears rolling down as she realizes that they're right. She wiggles around in her bonds, trying to get free, but to no avail. She whimpers and moans into her gag, wishing there was something she could do.

Then Kathy hears a plane coming in, hoping it's not for them. Of course though, it's the one the men are waiting for. They load her up, still throwing insults at her as they prep for take-off.

After three hours pass by one of the guys asks, "Which dock are we going to land at? It must be the one near his beach house."

"Yeah, that's the one the van's at."

When the plane lands and idles its way to the boat dock, the men grab her up and put her in the back of a van. Then they drive to the far side of town, into a warehouse. They get her out of the van and put her in a large room, under the floor with the others.

Kathy sits there for a little while, crying. Wondering about what's happening to her.

She hears another girl, "Hold on. Let me get that sack off your head." Slowly the girl pulls off the hood they had put on her and removes her blindfold.

Kathy's eyes slowly adjust to the dimly lit room. Kathy sits there, shivering from the fear of not knowing. She looks around and sees seven or eight girls, maybe even more hidden away in the corners of the room. Some of them look Spanish, or maybe from the United Kingdom. Most of them looked to be American. Almost all of them are bruised and battered; their eyes containing the fear of a beaten, caged animal. She begins talking to the girl sitting next to her, against the wall. "What happened? What is your name? My name is Kathy."

The girl looks up at her, "Aniline. When I was abducted, they gave me something to put me to sleep. When I woke up I was laying naked on the floor of the shower, with whip-bruising and severe pain inside. I was curled up in a fetal position. Cold water from the shower ran off down my head. As I went to move my head to look around, I noticed blood slowly trickling off of my leg. I had apparently been raped, by that Albanian man that had abducted me earlier in the night. But I was in a strange place that I had never seen before."

Aniline shuffles a bit closer to Kathy and puts an arm around her shoulder to try and comfort the poor thing. "Don't worry, they're not going to kill you. As I understand from listening to them we're going to be sold to someone at auction. I don't know what for. As much as I've heard we could be sold as house girls, doing anything under the sun, including cleaning. Or as prostitutes, laying on our backs for twelve to fifteen hours a day, making them a living. There's a lot of money to be made in prostitution."

Kathy turns her head to look up and notices a heavyset woman standing over her, cursing then and laughing maniacally as she begins whipping Aniline again with what looks like a TV cable. Aniline yells out as the cable strikes her, quickly moving away from Kathy and curling up to try and protect her face and body from the sinister beating. She grunts in pain every time the make shift whip bites into her skin, the woman above just laughing. "Y'all shut the fuck up down there. I hear anymore talkin and the nex'un gets it even worser!"

Kathy learns later from the other girls that this is standard routine with them. "They whip us to make us obedient for the new owner. Ready for the next client. Whipping you in the shower will reduce the swelling of the welts. The swelling needs to go down."

Then the girl tells Kathy, "When I first came in, I put up quite a fight. They do this to break your spirit down," then she added, "I heard the abductors talking, saying they had you in an apartment in Galway city. You was number 20 their newest sex-trafficking victim. They said they see you walking six hours earlier down the street; 800km from North London."

Aniline went on in a quiet, hushed voice, "Originally from Romania, I moves there to start studying nursing. I had a part-time job, cleaning offices. And a second job waitressing at a nearby café, trying to save my money for my nursing books."

"I moved into a house just a few weeks earlier. All the rooms were rented out to different Eastern European girls. The landlord was also Romanian, but I felt close to the other girls like I was at home."

"A year later I had enough money saved up, and enrolled myself in the college. One day, around lunchtime, I decided to ease myself back to my little apartment just off campus, to get me a bite to eat before heading back to school. I had just left the house, when I felt someone grabbing me around my neck. I glanced my eyes around to look. I noticed a car with the back door open. He was shoving me into the backseat of the car."

"When I heard the door close, they drove off. I began kicking and screaming. Then the man in the backseat began strapping and hitting me on my head. As I began shifting my eyes around to look, I noticed a woman in the front seat. She turned around real fast and grabbed my bag with my cell phone, wallet and other things of importance. As I reached out to grab my bag to keep her from taking it, the man started hitting and slapping me on my head again, saying, 'Don't you say a damn word. We know where your family lives and we will kill all of them. We know who you are.'"

"Why didn't you try to escape the car or fight? And how did they know all of that about you?" asks Kathy while listening to the girl tell her story.

"Well, I realized there was no need of fighting. I didn't stand a chance. I just sat there, not saying a word. I eased just my eyes over to look at the driver. I recognized him. These two... they were both renting rooms in the house, along with me and the other girls."

"The lady in the front seat turned her head slightly towards me and told me where my parents both lived. They had a good description. Then she added, 'If you don't cooperate we will go back and kill them both.' I was petrified. I couldn't move or think straight. I even had a hard time swallowing."

Kathy says, "I thought this sort of thing only happens on the movies."

Chapter 5

"I have read about people like this. I've heard tales, stories of people going missing, never to be seen again. It has never been in my nature to be around people that were corrupt in any fashion." Aniline let out a deep breath as she spoke in a quiet tone. "I sat there, thinking about what they said; killing my parents. I began to shake inside and got sick to my stomach with my nerves."

"I began looking out the window as we were pulling into London Luton Airport. The lady reached up over the sun visor and grabbed airplane tickets, then she turned her head 'Get out. Get out the car.' While we were getting out of the car she said, 'Remember I told you. Not a word. You won't get second chance. Don't try to be hero. You'll get you and you parents killed.'"

"The driver dropped us off in front of the airport and drove off. We entered on into the lobby, and I heard an announcement, 'Boarding flight to Galway.' I turned my eyes to look at the lady. She looked relieved."

Kathy blurted out, "At least then you knew where they're taking you?"

The girl shook her head slowly, biting her lip. "That didn't matter, there was nothing I could do anyway. I just sat there with the lady and her coworker in the lobby. Confused and scared. Somewhat puzzled. What to do? I needed to think of a way to escape. Using a shallow voice, 'I've got to go to the bathroom. I've gotta pee.' He turned his head toward me and said with a deep, shallow, scraggly voice, "Sit there and be quiet. You can use the bathroom on the plane.'"

"I said, 'I can't hold it that long. When I've gotta pee, I've gotta pee.'"

Stroking the girl's hair slowly to comfort her, Kathy asks, "Didn't you see any police in the airport?"

"I frantically looked around to see if I could find somebody like a security guard, anybody that would have some kind of authority to help me. But there was no one to be found. Where's a cop when you need one?"

"We heard on the intercom that it was time to board the flight to Galway. We was sitting in the lobby. The lady reached down into my purse bag and pulled out my ID. The man stood up and reached down, grabbing me under my arm. He led me over to the line, boarding for Galway. We were slowly inching up toward the ticket clerk. Should I say something? But it may risk my family getting killed. Then she handed the ticket to the flight attendant. He looked at my ID and looked back up at me. Then he handed it back to the lady. I could feel something round, pushing into my side. I didn't know if it might be a gun or not."

"The one thing I did know, was that the flight attendant was not alarmed. Nor did he feel it was strange, someone else handing my ID to him. He didn't think it was strange or peculiar. I was hoping he would notice something strange and start asking questions. The man and the woman that had me, were very calm and collected. They knew everything was going to be okay, going through here."

With wide eyes Kathy asked "Didn't it seem strange to anyone on the plane that you were being escorted? I'm sure you weren't the only person there. Couldn't anyone help you?"

"Well, when we boarded the plane, there wasn't many people going to Galway. The lady stepped into the row of seats first, then the man shoved me in and sat down next to me. Most people probably thought we were a family. Father, mother and daughter. I kept my head straight, looking forward. Out of my peripheral view I could see the man's eyes fixed on me. Making sure I didn't move."

"I thought when we land in Galway Airport and make our way out front, I might could run and find a taxi... or even maybe board a bus to get away. But when we landed at the gate near the plane there were two Romanian men that were dressed like pimps, one of them looked like someone I've seen in the newspaper that was facing serious charges on the continent."

"I could hear one of the men talking quietly to the other saying, 'How much did we give again for her? €20,000, which would be 23,000 give or take in US dollars.' Then the other guy said, 'Money well spent. She a perfect candidate to fit in the trafficking circle. We will make a lot of money back on her. Some of the men will ask for her by name. You will see.'"

Kathy thinks to herself Aniline is a bit on the slim side. She's very attractive. Not just in her face, but her body also. And then, the big blue eyes she has. They just draw you into her.

Aniline continues, "I heard the woman saying that I don't have any family in London that would be concerned about me disappearing. They said it would be easy to smuggle me out from there."

"After the plane landed, we exited the airport and made our way to the car, and was headed down the road, and driving for some time. Then I noticed a city limit sign saying Salthill. We rounded the corner of a few streets and drove up to a house that sits conveniently behind a bunch of buildings. The man opened the door to the car, then reached back and grabbed me under the arm and pulling me out of the car. Now, walking very fast up to the house and through the doorway, I went inside where I met a madam, who I later learned ran the brothel there. I didn't know then, but this lady was going to make my life a living hell for the next several months."

"When we begun walking our way through the house I turned to the lady and said, 'I am very hungry. Can you give me something to eat and drink?'"

"One of the men grabbed me and punched me in the face. When I fell and hit the floor, he knelt down on me, beating me in the back. 'Do you know what you got to do for food? You don't eat until afterwards.'"

"When the man got up off of my back, the madam started ripping my clothes off of me, just like she was in anger. I could see it written across her face, but I knew I had done nothing to her for this. Then she grabbed a knife from the kitchen and cut off what clothes I had left covering my body. She just left me laying there, naked, in front of the men. They begin to laugh as it is funny to them. I tried to try to cover my chest and my crotch with my hands and arms, pushing myself back into the corner of the room."

"I began to say I want to go home. They laugh out louder saying, 'You can't get out here. We are watching you close. But don't worry. In a few minutes, your new boyfriend is going to show up. He will take care you. He got take care you all right. He's got have sex with you. Then you can get some food, something to eat and drink. There will be lots of other new boyfriends coming. They can help you get something to eat, too. Only if you do what they say. No trouble from you. We're a family now, and Baby, you will help pay the bills.' Then, with a serious look on her face, the madam said, '...and you can only pay the bills if you have a lot of boyfriends every day. Then we can ALL eat.'"

"After a few minutes, while I was still sitting in the corner naked, I heard the front door of the house open. I turned my head. There was an Albanian man that walked in from outside. I turned my head back around. The madam was walking toward me. I flinched and ducked and I began peeking under my arm to see what was gonna happen. She walked over to greet him. I could hear them talking, 'Here's your money'. He handed her an envelope. I later learned that there was €200 (which is $274 US currency) in that envelope. The madam came back through the doorway. She tossed the money over to one of the pimps sitting in the chair."

As Aniline told her story she began to cry. Still petting her hair with one hand, Kathy reaches out with the other to wipe her tears away softly with her thumb.

"I lifting my head up from under my arms and proceed to look through the doorway of another room. The Albanian man was laying naked on the bed. He hollered out to the madam, 'Where's my girl? For all the troubles I go through for this household, where is my pleasure?' Then the madam came back from the bedroom, storming her feet down on the floor, heading into the kitchen. She reached over for my hand and grabbed me by my hair, lifting me up to my feet. She hollered directly in to my ear, 'Move. Move, now; you stupid bitch! Get yor ass in the bedroom with yor master. He got to train you for yor future. Don't give me no troubles. I get that knife and see how much more deep I can cut. Not just yor clothes this time!'"

"The madam dragged me into the bedroom by the head of my hair. I hollered out. 'Stop! Leave me alone!' Then I cried, slapping at the lady's hand on my head. The madam finally dragged me into the bedroom, closing the door behind her. Then she pushed me down on the bed, letting go of my hair. The Albanian rolled up to his knees from laying down, with his Johnson hanging down between his legs. He grabbed me by the arms and slid them under his knees. Then he began punching me on my back. "Lick my dick," swinging down near my nose.

"A few more minutes of him beating me on my back and I finally gave in. I started caressing the head of his dick with my mouth. After a few more minutes, it had become to be stiff. Stiffer than anything I've ever seen. Then he rolled over and got off of my shoulders. He reached down and grabbed me by the arm, pulling me up toward the headboard. I hollered and screamed from fear of what he was going to do with his oversize, extracting dick. He began popping me in the face with his open hand, until I began to feel blood on the bottom side of my lip."

"After another minute or two, I just laid there. I was worn out and exhausted. I didn't have another fight in me. I didn't have enough energy to save my life if I needed. I could feel my legs being pushed up toward my chess. Then I could feel him pushing it in me. I felt like my stomach was going to cave in. Then the real pain began. Extraordinary pain. Then... I just passed out."

Kathy put her arm around the girl and pulled her in close, letting Aniline cradle her head between her neck and shoulder. She started to gently pet her cheek, feeling her own fear build up as she realized soon she would be in for her own horror.

"Some time it passed, I don't know how long. There was not a clock in sight. The windows were boarded up. As I reached my hands out I could feel the bed sheets beneath my fingers. Then I heard the door hit the back of the wall as it was flung open."

Chapter 6

"As I looked for all the strength I could find to lift my head up, I could see it was the madam. She was hollering, 'Get up. Go to the shower. Go to the shower, now. You stupid little bitch. I'll fuck you with that knife, and see how you like it." Then she reached over and grabbed me by the hair. I began to think, 'that must be her favorite spot to grab.' Then she dragged me out of bed. I quickly put my feet beneath me onto the floor. She began pulling me out of room and down the hallway. I stumbled behind her. Then faster than a frog takes a shit, she pushed me into the shower and turned the water on. Setting it hot. I tried to roll out of the way of the water. When I turned around trying to get away from her, she reached round grabbed the TV cable and began whipping me until I finally stood up and got into the back corner of the shower, trying to get away from her. A few moments later, she turned off the water, grabbed a towel and threw it at me. I wrapped myself up in it."

"Then the madam grabbed her favorite spot again. She began pulling me back down the hallway. She snatched me up under the arms and dragged me to my feet. I could hardly walk, as my feet tripped over one another, making our way into the room. She pushed me down onto the small mat on the floor. Wasting no time, the madam pulls the door and locks it."

"I cried until I couldn't cry anymore. I was too scared to get angered. The only thing I did know was I want to try to live, hoping I would have the choice in that at least."

Again tears fell down Aniline's face, a low sob coming from her. "Shhh...you're still alive, dear, and we'll make it out of here somehow." Kathy kept trying to console her, thumbing her tears away and petting her hair. She didn't know if she believed herself though. "Just continue on with your story..."

Aniline nods, wrapping her arms around Kathy's waist in a soft hug. "After a little time, I began to get rebellious. If I asked for anything, even if it was just food, they would beat me down onto the floor. They would hit me in the head with their fist. Push me into the wall. And when I was laying down on my bed in the room they gave me something to eat. If I was asleep, they would pour a glass of water on me to wake me up. I think they were trying to break me. You know, break my spirit. They want us to do anything they say just like a robot."

"They had boards nailed up over most of the windows. The living room had blinds but they were always pulled down. And even though I couldn't see the outside, I could hear the cars passing. In the mornings would be the loudest, when the cars would pass headed to work."

"I thought eventually, if I played along with the madam's men, they would begin to like me and be kind. But that wasn't going to happen."

"All they were interested in was Madam's satisfaction that I keep a steady income coming into the house. It's always the money. That's what pleasured them the most.

"After I had been there a couple days, they began to bring me into my room, locking the door behind them. I would see up to twenty-two men a day. Some were stinking drunks, stopping by after leaving the bar. Some would come in straight from work, not shower. Stinking. You'd almost throw up your stomach. From time to time, some who were good businessman, smelled good from their aftershave. But, I was never allowed to go anywhere."

"Sometimes, I was allowed to walk up into the living room. I'd sit down on one of the three couches, but the front door remained locked, with the key. As I would sit there, I would look over at the lamp table on the other side of the room and see four cell phones. The Albanian man would be sitting right next to them. It seemed to be his job to answer any of them if they rang. Some of the calls I'm sure were new clients for me or one of the other girls locked away in their room. Sometimes the phones would ring late up into the night, looking for someone to have sex with. Then one of us girls may get woke up at 2 o'clock in the morning to have sex with some stranger. Sometimes it was a regular client."

"If I was sitting in the living room I'd see that when a client would come out of one of the other girls' rooms, the Albanian would be sitting at their front door. The client would pay him between €70 and €200. That's almost $96 and $254, depending on what he wanted the girl to do and for how long. If the Albanian was not in the living room, the money was given to either the madam or one of the pimps. As much is I hate to admit it, for making money, they are in the right business."

"After what could have been a couple months or so, I could no longer keep up with the days. Two of the girls were taken to another brothel, in the heart of the town, called Belfast City. It is run by two pimps."

"A couple days had passed, some new clients came through. I think they were police officers and I think they were married. It was easy to tell with the rings still on their fingers."

"A week or so after that we were raided by the police. They took in the two pimps, but none of the girls were arrested. I felt that that was kinda strange, but go figure. A few minutes after the raid, the Albanian man showed up and took us back to Galway, from where we came from. I felt so low. I hated it there. I liked it better where we were. I kept thinking, 'How can I kill myself? I really don't want to live any longer.' When I would try to hide in the storage closet, they would find me, torture me, then punish me."

"I began to try to make friends with the other girls. I found out that, some of them were watching me close. If I did anything wrong, one of the girls would tell Madame. If I said anything about running, in return they would get drugs for their reward. Sometimes, they would just make up some things, then I would get dragged to the shower by my hair and whipped with a TV cable cord, until I couldn't stand up. After a while I figured, I might as well play along."

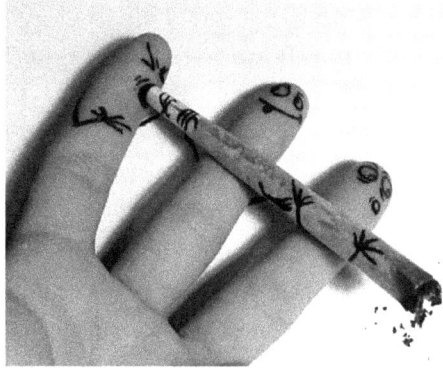

"One day, when it was being busy, I was sitting in the living room. The madam walked through the door, 'I want you answer the phone. Take down numbers new clients. Set up times the regular clients. You understand me? Don't try anything sneaky. I have ways find out.'"

"Our busiest time of the year was during the Galway horse races. That is what pulls in a lot of money here. But during one racing season we were raided by the gardai, which are police. Me and three other girls were arrested and charged for working in a brothel. However the Albanian, the madam, and their two pimps never got arrested."

"I really wanted to tell the guard or somebody how I got there, but with all the commotion going on, I didn't get the opportunity. They didn't want listen to me. They treated me very trashy. So on court day, I pleaded guilty and someone paid my fine for me to be released. Come to find out it was the Albanian man."

"When me and the other two girls walked out the front doors of the police station, the pimps were out on the streets, waiting for us. They grabbed us and put us in the car. We drove for a little ways and it began to get dark. I gazed out the front windshield. I could see a sign coming up as the headlights glanced upon it. It was Cork City. We continued on into town, turning street corners. I noticed another road sign. Western Rd. By the time we got settled in, a month had passed. Then the madam told me to grab all my things, "Go out. Get in the van. Be fast. Don't make me look for you.' I did exactly as I was told, too scared not to."

"After a few hours of driving down the highway, we came to the little city of Limerick. We pulled down a little narrow road, to a house sitting off way back in the background. Several days went by. The madam would come and go from the house, as her pimps kept an eye on us. They constantly pleasured themselves with us. Sometimes doing a threesome. To my surprise the madam said, 'pack your things and get in van.' I was beginning to think they're on the run. They're always moving one step from the law. On the island of Ireland, they can keep an eye on us and we can't run far."

"Then I seen a new city sign. Dublin. As we continued on into town, the madam pulled into a hotel. Then I heard a plane flying over. After another minute or two, I could hear one taking off. I realized we must be near an airport."

"When the madam came back out to the van she told the pimps that were watching us that she had rented several rooms in the hotel. She handed the keys and the numbers to them and told them to take us on upstairs. We climbed several flights of stairs. I kept looking for a way out. We made it up to the third-floor. Then walked down the corridor, toward some rooms at the end. I looked around. There were no stairways."

Chapter 7

Aniline takes a few deep breaths, her body shaking. It must had been hard for her to have to remember just painful things. "Just about everybody, in one way or the other, talks about sex. Some like it. Some don't like other people liking it. Then they condemn it."

Kathy looks at Aniline concerned, "So, I guess now we're in the business of sex?" and then after Aniline nods, "Where were you headed next? Continue your story."

"The next day, after we all got settled into our rooms. One of the pimps came to the door and unlocked it. All he did was open it up and look in then pulled it back, but the door did not latch. It opened up just a little bit, leaving a crack. I figured he was just checking on me. I looked out the crack of the door. I could see they had set up a small table and chair a little ways down, past the rooms. The other pimp was sitting at the table. The only thing I could gather was so they can keep a good eye on us while also look for new clients coming from the airport. They take the money at the table, just like running a carnival and the customers can go for a ride."

"The main thing we would get out of it, would be more drugs. No money. No freedom. Sex and more drugs. Either one is not too bad, if you can enjoy it on your own time. If you like the person you're doing it with. Of course, I remember where I come from. I was always hungry. Lots of poverty. Sometimes we would not have a good roof over our head. It would be no more than a big piece of cardboard and several sheets of rusty tin."

"It did appear to be a better set up. Most of the clients were clean businessman. Sometimes a politician would fly in. And even occasionally a barrister. At least all of these were from the upper side of life. They were independent and proud of their lives. Sometimes they would lay there afterwards just for a moment and share with me, a little bit about them."

Kathy was trying to seem interested but honestly, she was getting scared, realizing that this is now her new life. "I'm not so sure I'd be comfortable talking with them. What would we talk about?"

"Well, some of them would share their name. They knew the information probably wasn't going to go anywhere. Some would say, 'If I could get you out from here, I'd set you up in your own place. We would really enjoy life together.' And things like that, of course I would not reveal anybody's name. It would be too risky for them and me."

"All I can say is I've spent half my life in the sex trade, and those eight months in the hotel have probably been the more rewarding time of it. That place was far better than where we came from at the brothel house. There, all we got was a stained up mattress and a shit pot in a room."

"Then one day without even realizing it… I don't know when, the crying, the pain and suffering slowly slipped away."

"Then one day the madam came into my room and told me to get my things ready. She left then came back with a needle, shot me up with something. Then I woke up here."

Kathy listens to Aniline tell her story. Not knowing how to handle being in this situation, she thinks to herself, "I need to find out more." Looking back at her new friend, "Nice talking to you."

Kathy stands up and walks over to one of the other girls that she sees sitting in the other corner of the room. She wants to hear her story as well. As she gets closer, Kathy notices, the girl is still crying. Kathy sits sit down next to her. She has long, dark brown hair running down her back. A dark complexion. Slender built and medium height. She lifts her head and turns to look at me. Then I notice her jade green eyes, sparkling from the light reflecting off of her tears. She flinched away from me, "You don't have to worry. I'm here with you. What is your name? My name is Kathy, what is yours?"

"My name is Amunet. I'm just so scared. I have been mixed up in this for a while, and too scared run, for what they may do to my family."

Kathy asked, "How did you get here? Where you from?"

"I'm originally from Alexandria, Egypt. I've been trafficked around so much. I even ended up in California close to my eighteenth birthday, but I don't even know where we are, anymore."

"Me and my brother and my sister was living in Alexandria with our mom and dad. That Monday morning when they kidnapped me I had gotten up, got dressed, did my hair, sat at the table and ate breakfast with my family. I told everybody to have a good day, grabbed my books and headed out the door, looking forward to my walk to school."

"I always liked school and was excited about getting there that morning, and seeing all my friends. I was popular. I got along with everybody and they got along with me."

"That afternoon, after school, I was walking up to the apartments and I seen somebody watching me, walking in opposite direction. I made it upstairs. No one had made it home yet so I unlocked the door. Then went ahead and got my homework done."

"As I was standing there, I heard the doorbell. I thought it might've been my little brother, trying to get in because I locked the door behind me. When I opened the door up, I seen it was my old boyfriend Chaths. He asked could he come in. With him was his friend, Haji. He had a reputation for prostituting local girls."

"Chaths asked me, 'What are you doing?'"

"'Give me a minute. I was right in the middle of doing something.'

"'I just wanted to invite you to a barbecue.'"

"'I can't. I've got homework.'"

"Then Chaths started looking at me with anger. He began to scare me, just a little bit. Then he reached up, grabbed me by the hair and pushed my head into the cabinet door. As I was standing there holding my head, not sure what I could safely say, I looked up. I could see Chaths grabbing my purse off the table. Then he reached down and grabbed my cell phone, then my jacket off the back of the chair."

"I began to put my jacket on. I could see him walking over to my chest-of-drawers. He opened up the top drawer and grabbed my passport."

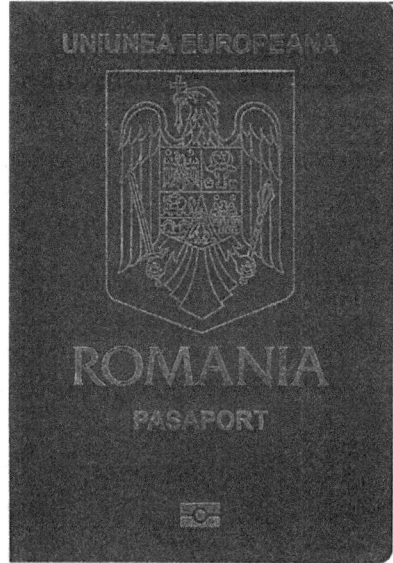

"'How did you know it was there? And what you needing it for?'"

"His friend Haji came over and grabbed me by the throat, pulling my head back and putting something flat up against my throat. Because of the cold, my guess is a knife. 'Let's go to that barbecue and have a good time now.'"

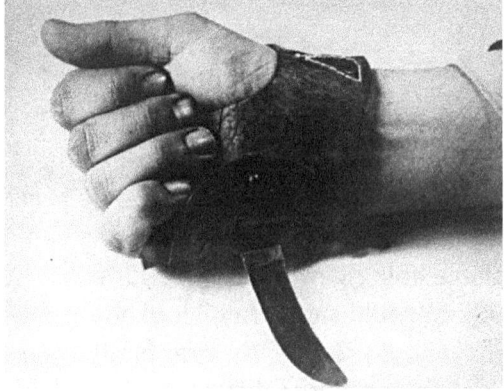

"We drove for a little while and it began to get dark. We were headed out of Alexandria. After driving for a couple hours, I could see a sign up a head. When the headlights glared across it, Kafr Galo. I knew at this point, I was a long ways from home. 'I said I want to go home!'"

"Chaths was driving the car. Haji turned around, 'Shut the fuck up, bitch; before I knock your teeth out.'"

"I was so shocked that Chaths do something like this. I fold into myself and try not to cry, holding myself in the back seat. Hoping and praying Haji would not make good on his threat."

"When we got into the city limits, they turned down quite a few streets. I did not know where I was. Then turned the steering wheel and pulled into a driveway."

Chapter 8

Amunet let out a sigh, then continued on in a low voice, still keenly aware of the sadists up above them. "He pulled up under the carport off to one side of the house. When I looked out the window it looked like a rent house, considering how trashy the yard looked. The house itself needed to be painted. When Haji got out of the passengers door, he reached back and grabbed me by the hair, pulling me out of the car. He was almost dragging me, as my feet were tripping over one another, as we walked to the back door of the house. After he unlocked it, he pulled me inside while Chaths was pushing me from the back."

"We made it into the first room. It looked like a very old kitchen. He pulled me into one of the small rooms coming off of the kitchen. There was a mattress on the floor and the windows were boarded up. Chaths stayed in the room with me, while his friend pulled the door behind us and locked it from the outside.

"Chaths started grabbing and pulling my clothes off. 'Look. You don't want to do this. This is not like you.' I was crying hard, not believing this was happening to me."
"I try to fight him, slap his hands away, to move away from him. He swung hit me in a nose. I fell down, I believe across the bed. As I lay there, holding my nose, I couldn't see anything. Everything gone dark."
"I could feel him as he pulled my panties off and rolled me over, onto my own stomach. I hollered out 'Don't do this.' He took his fist and hit me again harder, upside my head. Everything started to go blank. I could feel him pushing my knees under me."
"I could hear the sound of his zipper. I could hear his pants hit in the floor. He began to rub my butt with his hand. 'Please, don't do this.' I was pleading with him, bawling my eyes out practically. But he slapped my butt cheek hard, it began to tingle. He ran his fingers through my hair, grabbing it. He was making a hard fist and pulling my hair back toward him, until my neck began to hurt. I began to feel pain in my anal, as he was beginning to push his self into me."

"The pain was more than I can endure. I tried to move and couldn't with his weight down on me, then felt something warm in me. He came in me. It felt nasty. Very horrified. Deceived. I was really thinking that he would let me go home after he got through, but when he pulled out of me I heard a knock on the door. I heard him zipping his pants. I rolled over to look and heard Chaths' voice say, 'You're going to sleep with Haji tonight.' Then I heard the door close and lock once again."

"That night the door open once again and Haji raped me all night long. He made me do disgusting things. And if I didn't do them, he would hit me in the face."

Kathy inches herself closer to Amunet and gently wraps her arms around the poor girl. Pulling her in close she takes her in a warm embrace, trying to help her feel better. "My God...the things you've been through..."

"The next morning he got up, getting dress and banging on the door to be let out. Laying there with confusion on my mind and how this happened I began to think to myself, 'I'm sure my family is worried. They have probably already checked for me at the school and talked to my closest friend. But there's no way they will find me way over here.'"

"I begun trying to think of plots of escape. They wouldn't allow me to go outside the house or even out of the room. They put a bucket over in the corner for me to use the bathroom in. I even have to eat in this room."

"After a couple weeks of being raped repeatedly every day one day the door opened up. Chaths handed me some clothes and a brush for my hair. Chaths hollered, 'Put them close on and fix that hair. I'll be back for you in a minute. Be ready.' I got dressed and brushed my hair fast I begun feeling jittery inside from excitement, knowing I'll be seeing my family soon and be out of this hellhole. 'They are probably fixing let me go back home,' but after about five or 10 minutes pass he came back to the door, I could hear him unlocking it, he walked over and grabbed me on the arm. Pulled me through the door and walked me out into the kitchen, keeping his hand on my arm. Then he showed me my new passport, making me to be an older adult."

"They were driving me to the bus station. Haji said, 'If you talk to anybody or give any idea to anybody what's going on, I will go back and kill your family. I will tell them it's your fault, why they are dying. Do you understand?' He reached back and grabbed me by the hair behind my ear and shook

a little bit. I have to admit, he scared the hell out of me."

"When we got to the bus station, me and Chaths got out to wait on the bus. When the bus got there, me and Chaths got aboard. I noticed the ticket said to Romania, Bucharest."

"We got off the bus. A much older woman walked over to where we were standing and began talking to Chaths. She claimed to be Hajis friend, and said, 'We need to go.'"

"We all made our way to the car. I was looking out the side window from the back seat. It looked like we were driving outside of town. The woman turned onto a local road off to the right. It was very bumpy and only had two paths for the wheels to roll on. We started down a big hill then I saw the house. We finally made our way down there to the house and I began to feel very insecure. I could not come up for plan on how to get out of this. I may have to play along until I get my chance."

"The three of us walked in the house. I saw two girls sitting on the couch that look Romanian. The lady said her name is, '...Dendera and welcome to our happy little home. This is your new room.'"

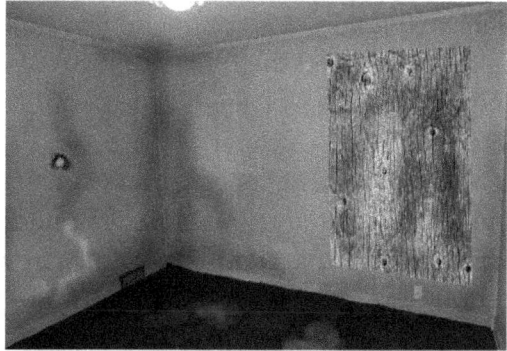

"Chaths pushed me over to the room, then pushed me inside. They pulled the door closed and locked it. It was the same set up as the other house. Boarded up windows, a peapod in the corner and a very heavily soiled mattress, laying on the floor. I didn't want sit on it. I just walked over to the corner of the room and leaned my back up against the wall. I really didn't want to touch anything; it was so nasty."

"I could hear the keys jingling, then the door opened up. I snatched my head around to look. A very nasty looking man walked in. He was short and very wide with a full beard, and he was bald. His clothes looked like they hadn't been washed in weeks. I could smell him from where I was standing in the back of the room."

"Then Dendera said, 'This is your first client. Do him right and you will live tonight.' Then she pulled the door behind her. I could hear the key locking."

"'The only way this guy was going to touch me was he was going to have to beat me down. God, he had a horrific smell, that would even kill flies. He began to walk over to me. I walked over to the other corner of the room. As he was walking to that corner, I went to the next. He continued to follow me around the room, 'Come on. Come to Daddy. You know I'm gonna catch you,' using a cheerful voice, like he was playing a game of cat and mouse. 'I wonder, who is the cat and who is the mouse?' As we continue to go around the room, I begin to get dizzy. I was hoping that he would get dizzy... and pass out."

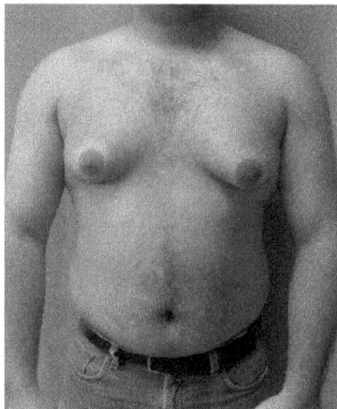

"Then he got up close to me, grabbing me by my arm and slinging me down on the bed. The first thing that jumped up in my head was, 'What could be worse than landing on that disgusting bed... or him touching my arm.' I rolled and came back to my feet. And as he grabbed for me I pushed, and we both fell backwards with myself on top of him. I quickly jumped my feet. Luckily, I had a soft landing, being how big he was."

"As he was picking himself up off the floor, getting his balance, he turned to me with both of his arms sprawled out like a bear, 'Come on, little bunny. I'm going to eventually catch you. My friend Dendera said I could have you for the night, but only if I break you in real good.'"

"He continued to chase me around the room, from one corner to the other. I was running past a small hole in the wall. I could hear two people giggling. I continued on to the next corner. My foot tripped on the mattress and I fell on top of him. We had been running around the room for a couple of hours. I was so tired. I went to roll to get up but I could feel his weight pulling down on me, like a giant walrus."

"He began tearing my shirt off and ripping my bra. I kept trying to slap him in the face, but my hands ended up slapping his bald head. He had his mouth down on my breasts, sucking on a nipple. I began to feel sick at my stomach. I wasn't sure if I was going to throw up or not. He reached up and grabbed my head and began kissing me on my lips. I tried to scream. It was impossible with his big, fat lips covering mine. All came out was muffled sounds in his mouth. I could hear the giggles coming from the hole in the wall, but I did not feel embarrassed. I felt nasty. He continued trying to kiss me for a couple of minutes, then he went back down to my breasts, sucking on the other nipple."

"I got to thinking, 'Maybe this is all he's going to do. I'm sure he had to look like a giant baby laying on me, sucking on my breast. I had a full set up breasts.' Then I thought, 'He's trying to make me feel hot and horny. I'm not as concerned, if this is the only thing he is going to do. I could lay here and deal with it.'"

A single tear rolled down Amunet's cheek as she continued on with describing her terrible ordeal. "As he was sucking on my breasts, things took a turn for the worse. He had shoved me down, so I could not move. He took his two hands and reached down to undo my pants. I tried to pull his hands off of me, but I could not move them. He was too big."

"There was a tap on the door, someone asking, 'Are you going to fuck that girl are not?'"

"'I will. I'm enjoying myself in here.' He continued pulling on my pants zipper. He lifted himself up onto his knees. I continued to fight and slap at him, hitting him in the chest and slapping him across the face. He continued pulling my pants down. He finally got them down to my knees, and said, 'Oh yeah. I like them butterfly panties. I'm fixing to grab me a butterfly.'"

"I grabbed the top of my panties and held on tight curling my fingers through the opening. He continued to pull my pants off, until they were off my ankles. I jumped up."

"I ran over to the corner of the room, trying to cover my breast up with my arms. I still had my panties on. Then I seen him raising to his feet. His face looked very angered. He threw his arms into the air and growled like a big bear. As I was watching him, he looked like a different person. Then he reached down and unzipped his pants. They dropped to the floor. His boxer underwear were all stained up, with urine stains. Maybe a few fart stains. He reached down and slid his boxer shorts off to the floor."

Chapter 9

Kathy tried to console the frail girl just like she had Aniline, petting her hair softly. She didn't really want to hear the rest of the story, but if it helped the girl to get this out then she would listen. She felt sorry for her, wishing there was something she could do about their current situation.

"I continue to run to the next corner, I noticed the hole in the wall and somebody was giggling in the other room. Turned back around to see what he was doing now. As shocking as it sounds, at that point I wasn't near as worried anymore. He had a little dick. Wasn't much bigger than a hot dog that came out of the microwave after being cooked too long. He was so nasty looking and I wasn't getting used to the smell."

"Then the giggles started up again. I looked around the floor and noticed a sheet of paper. I grabbed it, slid down the wall to where the hole was, and shoved the paper in the hole, he was enough to deal with without them watching and laughing."

"The burly bear lunged at me. I kept running from corner to corner. Then, as I was coming out of one the corners, I tripped on his old boots. I took a dive, head first, down into the bed. And down fell the giant walrus, back on top of me."

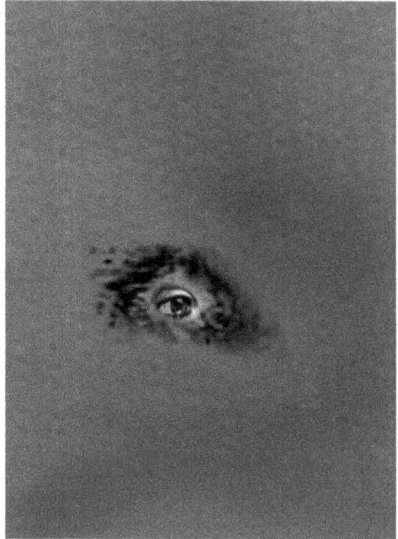

"He laughed, 'I told you I'd get you, little bunny.' As he was holding my chest down with one hand, he began ripping my panties off. Then he took his other hand and fondled me. Playing with me. Then he took his other finger and rubbed my anal, sliding the finger up inside. Then he took his thumb and ran it down into my crotch. He began pulling his fingers together. I started to scream. I was so uncomfortable and in pain. I don't need to go into any more detail. You know what happened. That was just the beginning of my life in hell."

Kathy nodded slowly, still holding the Egyptian girl. "It's okay, Honey, you don't have to tell me anymore than you want to. I know it must hurt to have to remember all of that."

"After a couple months passed, my list of clients grew to twenty men a day. I still could not find a chance to break away. I was missing my family a lot. I begun not to eat. I was withering away. My weight had dropped down a lot. I could see all my ribs. I was not much more than a skeleton frame."

The girl starts to sob again, letting her head fall into her knees. Kathy just gives her hair gentle strokes, letting her take all the time she needs. After a few moments of letting her pain be cried out she lifted her head back. "I could hear some keys jingling and someone turning the lock. The door to my room opened. Haji hollered out with a stern voice 'Get the few clothes you got, gather them up and stick them in a bag. We're going on a trip.'"

"That was the first time I'd felt excited in a while. I didn't know what was go on. I didn't know what was going to happen. The one thing I did know was I'm getting out this room. My opportunity to escape is greater. He come back for me. I had my little bag packed. We headed out the front door of the house and got in a suburban. Haji wasn't driving. I don't know who the driver was."

"I was looking out the side window and noticed it was beginning to get dark. As we got to the city limits, Haji pulled out his gun and put it my head. I nearly cried right there. I froze, too scared to move. 'Don't be a hero. I can take care of you and your family. You have the choice. Just play along. Things may get easier for you.' We were pulling into a bus station and he put his gun under his belt. We stepped out of the car. He already had tickets and the bus was already waiting. As we was walking up to the bus I looked above the windshield. The sign read 'London'."

"After several hours and many miles had passed, we finally made it to London. Then we continued on to Birmingham's central bus station. When we got out of the bus I seen Chaths signaling with his hand to come over to the car. When we got there, they talked some kind of gibberish; some code. As we continued on out of town I seen another sign; Edgbaston. We turned and went down several blocks. He finally pulled into a large, suburban house."

"When we walked in, there were two Romanian girls in the kitchen, making themselves a sandwich. Haji told the two girls to keep an eye out on me. Then Haji and Chaths went out the front door."

"One of the Romanian girls said to me, 'Do you know how to put on a condom?'"

"It took me a minute to realize what she just said. Then it dawned on me. 'Can you repeat that? What are you talking about? A condom?'"

"The other Romania girl laughs, 'She said, do you know how to put on a condom? We are going to go to a nearby brothel. It's more of a massage parlor. We need to make some money.'"

"No! I don't want to go!"

"The Romanian girl said, 'You know if you don't go; when Chaths gets back from Romania he may just go ahead and kill you. Then your family. He's not scared to kill. He's done it before.' One of the Romanians put me into a sealed off room, locking the door behind me. The two Romanian girls, scurried on off to the massage parlor to make some money for the house."

"The next day, Chaths and Haji showed back up at the house. The two Romania girls told them what I had said about the massage parlor."

"Haji opened up the door where I was locked up. Chaths came in the room and Haji locked it behind him. I got up from the bed and went and stood in the corner of the room. He walked over to where I was standing. Pushing myself back into the corner, he stepped within arm's reach of me, so I couldn't escape from the anger he was about to release on me. As I began to plead with him, he reached up and grabbed me hair. He slammed my head into the wall, then he punched me in the stomach, giving me three good blows. I fell to the floor."

"He reached down and unzipped my pants. Walking around where my ankles were he yanked them off. Then he unzipped his, dropping them to the floor. He reached over and grabbed me by the arm. I began to scream loud; I heard the giggling from the hole again. He drew back his arm, into the air. Then he came down with his hand with a hard force, slapping me across the face. My lip was bleeding. He turned around and grabbed me by the ankle, to drag me over to the bed. As I laid on my back, kicking and screaming at him, he took his foot and kicked me in the crotch. I rolled over into a fetal position and began to cry. He rolled me over onto my stomach. Then he took his knees and spread my legs apart. Then he had rough, dry, anal sex with me. This continued into the late night. When it was over, he eased his head over and whispered into my ear, saying, 'Next time the girls ask you to go make some money for the house, you do that. You go make money for the house.'"

"Haji and Chaths gave me a day to recuperate. Then Chaths unlocked the door and handed me a new outfit. It included a pink bra and panties, with white lace running around the outer edge. 'Go out with the girls tonight. Make some money for the house.'"

"I tried to have a cheerful smile and said, 'Okay. Anything. Just don't hurt me again.'"

"He replied, 'Next time, I will stay on top of that booty, until it really loosens up.'"

"The two Romanian girls and I left for the nearby brothel that doubles as a massage parlor. They all appeared to be in a spontaneous mood to have some fun and make money. One of the Romanian girls began to tell me about how much they have made. 'On the first day I made £300 which is $500 US. I got to thinking that's enough to feed my whole family for six weeks, back in Egypt. But after a couple days I started making £400, £500. After a month passed I was making £500 a day, easy. But it all has to go to the house. We keep none of it. If you want something to drink or something to eat, you have to ask the man you're fucking to buy it for you.'"

"'I said I can't say the English very well at all.'

"'You don't need to know English. Sex has its own language that's worldly known.'"

"When we finally made it to the massage parlor we walked in and over to the counter to make it known that we were there. We waited at the booth to be called to go on into the back and do a complete body massage, including the penis and anything else he wanted to be massaged."

"The girl at the counter motioned for me to come over. 'Take the men to the back,' she said. 'Your room will be number twelve.' When me and a new client made it into the room, he began undressing right away. Then he motioned for me to go ahead and undress. I wanted to say, no, but couldn't. I didn't know how, but tried to explain to him that I am involved with somebody that has trafficked me. Instead, I started crying, hoping that he would take pity on me. He didn't. I looked up at his face. All I could see is he wanted to have sex with me. The rest of the men didn't take pity either. Most of the men were Asian and white. Some were repeat clients. But for the biggest part of them were strangers. They could be drunk and a few were violent."

"The three of us began pulling shifts daily, twelve hours a day. From 10 PM to 10 AM. This continued on for seven days a week; and they were all different men. It was nothing unusual to get 10 men a day, paying £40 a session. This equals $67 US. But then the massage parlor got half. One of the Romanian girls began telling me story about one of the guys who asked her to do something she didn't want to do. 'He was drunk, so he beat me down good, then pulled my hair and slapping me like this,' she pretended to wallop the side of her face, like he did. She was doing it so hard, her head jerked until her tongue began to wag out of her mouth. 'They just take the drunk troublemakers, put them outside. They never call the law. Nothing ever happens to them. Even if I'm really hurt.'"

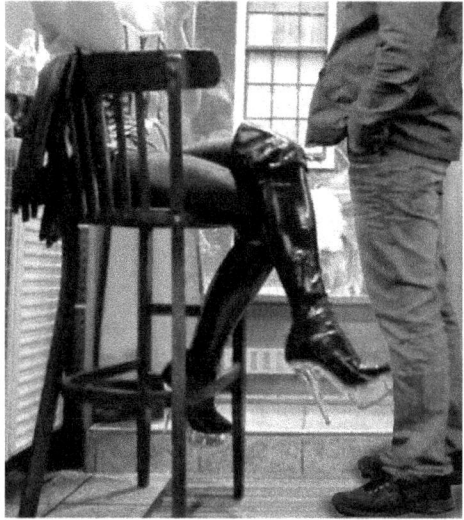

"It's almost traumatizing, having to undress for some of the stinkiest men that come straight from work. Some of them I don't think they showered in a week or two. When their smell gets on you it's hard to get it off. Then I have to expose those damn stupid-looking, horrifying underwear that Chaths make me wear. I'm supposed to be in high school; not in England having to sleep with all these nasty man and making money for criminals rapists!" Amunet's eyes flare in anger and her hands ball into fists as she says that, gritting her teeth tightly. Then, as if it never happened, she turns back to her sad self.

"Haji and Chaths gave orders to the massage parlor, 'Do not let the girls go outside.' Often this would last for days. But I tried to make an escape one day and when they caught me, they dragged me to the back room and called Haji. When he showed up, he gave me one of the most brutal beatings I ever had. I got a knife put to my head and my hair was pulled until it was coming out, leaving me with a humongous headache."

"Haji's girlfriend would scan through the classified section of the local newspaper and bring up any massage parlors or saunas she would see that had ads. She would call and ask them, 'Do you require any girls to work.' She was calling to see if they had any jobs available. Jobs is a code for brothels. Then the three of us would be transferred around to all the brothels and massage parlors along the West midlands. We even made our way around to Linda's Sauna in east Birmingham where a lot of girls work."

OUSTED KAISER FLEES TO HOLLAND

"After some time passed, two new Romanian girls were trafficked in. We had relocated to Edgbaston, but both of the girls had some severe mental problems. One was around the age of 23, but she had the mental capacity of a 10 year old girl. Both of them made very little money for the house and a pimps quickly sold them off."

Chapter 10

Amunet leans against Kathy, trying her best not to cry. Laying her head in the other girl's lap she lets out a deep breath. The only thing stopping her from breaking down right now was the gentle strokes upon her hair.

"Then they took me to work in Belle Air massage parlor. I worked there at least four to six months. It's really hard to keep up with the time. Then I went to Shangri-La and there was up to fifteen girls a day working in the brothels. My guesstimate, I probably have met more than a hundred Romanian girls working as prostitutes in Birmingham by itself. These girls said they were coerced into going and there is a large-scale off-street prostitution in Britain alone."

"One of the times that I got arrested, the sergeants told me (actually he read to me a report they had about trafficking), 'There's more sex trafficking going into the UK, than just about anywhere else, with over 5,890 brothels, saunas and massage parlors used for illegal paid sex in England and Wales."

"'Another report claimed they had found 342 brothels in the West Midlands. I was among the 1,535 east European women working in most of the sex parlors. They average six to ten beds. Another report said, 'In North West England, there was over 750 operations identified for hiring 1,242 sex workers from Eastern Europe."

"'In one more report he read, 'In the UK there was evidence that there was women from Eastern Europe who had been trafficked, but they say the true number is in the thousands.'"

"There is little evidence or any concern of police trying to crack down and close these operations."

Kathy replies, "That is really horrifying that somebody won't stop it. Maybe someday. If we live long enough. I'm gonna get up and walk around some. It was nice talking to you."

As Kathy begins walking across the room. She sees what appears to be a very tall, light skinned girl with long, wavy, dirty blonde hair. The girl looks up toward Kathy with a very lonely face. She is very young and beautiful. She is laying down on a cot and looks sick, like she may be having some drug withdrawals. Kathy walks on over and sits down on her cot next to her. "My name is Kathy. Are you okay?"

"My stomach hurts and I keep throwing up. My name is Anico and I am from a small village near Hungary. This is my second time being caught by traffickers. It is so depressing I have been robbed of my youth. They had mentally tore me down so much. I don't think I've got the mental strength to escape anymore. I'm afraid they have won this time. The first time I got away from the pimps I was 18. I had talked to the home office of Britain Immigration. They looked into my case about everything. I told them. They knew I was a part of the human traffickers and forced into doing prostitution, but the only help they gave me was to send me back home. The officer said I would not be in any danger. They're so full of shit. They may be a part of the trafficking ring. I could tell the British didn't treat the trafficking of women seriously."

"Just days after I got out of jail, they sent me back to the UK. The traffickers began looking for me and found me, back in the little village where I grew up. I was headed to the store, and some of them jumped out from the side of the building. Each one of them grabbed me and started dragging me to the street behind them and threw me in the car. They drove a great distance into the woods and drug me out of the car. Then they pushed me down the ground and they began gang raping me. I cannot believe I was going through this again. I screamed and hollered for help, "Please don't do this.' I was in so much pain, but my fear overcame the pain I was in. They were laughing and threatening me. Then they tied me around my neck, like you would a dog. One end of the rope was tied to the top of a small tree and the other end tied to my neck. The tree was pulling on me."

"The whole time they kept the gun on me. They went to the trunk of the car, pulled out a shovel, walked over toward me and threw the shovel down at my feet. 'Dig your grave, you stupid bitch. Trying to get us in trouble. This will teach you to run off.'"

"I began to dig. I couldn't stop shaking. I had a very hard time holding a shovel. One of them was very impatient and began to get angry at me, for not digging fast enough. He walked over and shoved me down on the ground. He put his knees on my shoulders, then one of the other guys held my head back and push my jaw open. Then pushing a stick down in my mouth across my jaw to keep it open, the one that was kneeling on my shoulders pulled out a pair of pliers and pulled out my front tooth."

Kathy's eyes went wide in horror. She understood that these mean were cruel and treated the girls like shit, but she had never expected such an act. She instantly threw her arms around the girl and brought her in close.

"My mouth begun to flood with blood, and I began to gag. I was afraid I was going to choke on my own blood. He got up off of my shoulders, then pulled me up on to my feet. I began to bend over from the pain. I looked out the corner of my eye, I could see him untying the rope from the tree. I was so scared I couldn't hardly stand up. Then I felt it beginning to rain. I felt the ropes snatch on my neck pulling me over to the car."

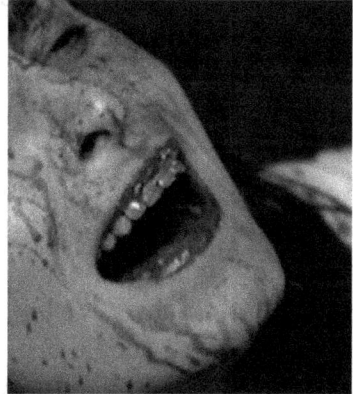

"He took the loose end of the rope, pulled my arms behind my back and tied them. Then he shoved me headfirst into the trunk of the car. I could feel him tying a rope around my ankles. I was so scared. I closed my eyes, hoping to make some of it go away. It was more than I could endure. Then I heard the trunk slam closed."

"For several days I had no knowledge of where I was at and where I was going to. I believe they kept me drugged so I would continue sleeping. They would give me bottled water but it tastes like something in it. But when you're thirsty, you will drink anything. I continued sleeping for some time."

"When I woke, I felt groggy. I don't know how long I slept. I could hear engines. I think I was on a cargo ship because we would rock from side to side. I could feel my stomach in pain from hunger. When they finally got me out of this big box I was in I heard someone say, 'Wake up.' I slowly turned my eyes to see who was talking. The man had walked away. I heard a door slam and some keys jingling as it locked."

"When I become back to my senses I looked around in the room. I could see a stained up bed over in one corner and a bucket in the other. Trash and paper on the floor. I began sifting through the papers on the floor, to try to get an idea of where I'm at. Then I seen a brochure. On the front of it read, 'Welcome to Israel.'"

"I was there several months. They would continue to let another man in the room almost every hour, up until the early morning. Most of the time I was so hungry and exhausted I would just lay there and fall asleep. Most of the men didn't care, but sometimes I'd be awoken with my face being slapped. When I would come to my senses there would be somebody laying on top of me, smelling like a sewer. At first I would begin to gag, like I was going to throw up, but then they would hit me hard on top my head with their hand saying, 'Don't do that. Don't even think about doing that, you stupid little bitch. When I get done fucking you in your ass, I gonna fuck your mouth, just like the dog you are.'"

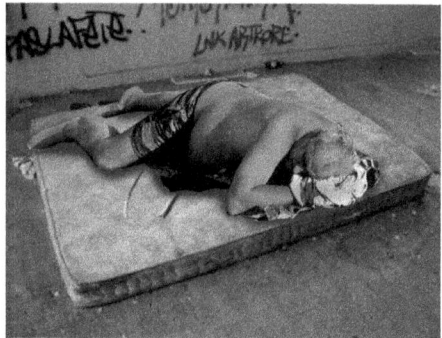

"A good bit of time had passed, then one of the pimps walked in, he had a syringe with something in it. I began to back into the corner of the room, scared for my life. As he would come to my corner I would run to another one. Then he hollered out for one of the other pimps. When the pimp came in the room they surrounded me in the corner. One of them held me up in the corner by my throat. I began to gag. The other one tied something around my arm. I began to feel my arm go numb. I could feel the pinch of the needle going into my vein. Then, shortly later, I passed out. I didn't regain consciousness for days."

"When I regain my conscience, I was in another room. Mattress on the floor and bucket in the corner. I could hear the jingle of keys, as someone was unlocking the door. When the door was pushed open I seen a familiar face. It was Madame. I worked for her before. That's how I knew I was back in the UK."

Chapter 11

"I was fourteen years old when I first came to this house. They sold me to a pimp, who sold me to another pimp. This continued on for more than six years. I was forced to do prostitution in several countries. I had been in Italy, Turkey, Israel, Romania, Hungary, and then back in the UK."

"Years ago when I got picked up by the police for prostitution, I told the guardian that was over the British police that they need to do more to help protect women from pimps like that. Stop the trafficking. But all I would get were negative looks from them. As if I really wanted to be out there. One or two, looked like clients. They would look at us like we're making all the money and this is a business we enjoy."

"I continue to talk to the police chief, 'Just open up your damn eyes. You can see them, there in the tube station (underground subway). I know I can recognize them and I'm sure you can if you would try. Shut down the brothels and the saunas. Then there would be no more pimps and no more prostitution. We could go home and try to have a life for ourselves. Why can't you see that? You're just not trying.'"

"I continued to plead with him. He would just sit there and say nothing. 'As many times as I have been through here and charged for prostitution, I have given you the names and places in all the court documents. I told you how I was targeted. How I was captured and intimidated for my life. I told you all the methods. How these gangs are involved with trafficking vulnerable women from East Europe, to Africa, all the way to the Far East. I know you can see the danger we are in when your British immigration service comes to remove us.'"

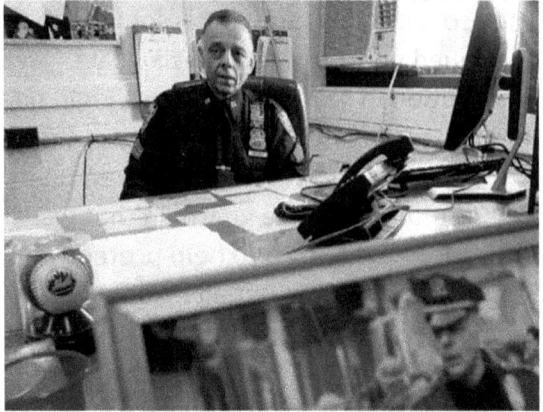

"On one occasion, the officer turned and gave me a concerned look. 'We know all about it and believe it or not, we are trying to do something.' He handed me a report and I began to read it to myself. It read: 'The Poppy Project was set up in 2003, to provide high-quality support, advocacy and accommodation to trafficked women; that is, women who have been brought into England or Wales to be exploited in some way. This could include, but is not limited to, sexual exploitation, labor exploitation, forced illicit activities and organ harvesting. Support workers work with women to create individual support plans for them, which can include financial help, support accessing health services and treatment, specialist counseling, criminal and immigration-related legal advice, education and employment opportunities and other support as needed.'"

"They sent me to talk to a counselor. After the counselor asked me several questions and had begun profiling me, she turned and said, 'You have one of the most disturbing stories I have ever heard and you are showing that you are suffering from post-traumatic stress disorder.' I could not tell her anymore. It was just too painful to continue talking."

"I will tell you like I told her. I had just turned 14 years old and was living with my mother. I didn't have much supervision from my parents. One night a week before I had met these two nice-looking men down on the street corner. I was telling them tomorrow is my birthday. One of the guys went to hand me a cigarette. 'We will throw you a birthday party. Come back down to this corner tomorrow, before lunchtime. That will give us enough time to put it together."

"Then I ask them, 'Can I Bring a girlfriend of mine?'"

"He replied, 'Yes, that would be nice.'"

"The next day, I was excited that someone cared enough to throw me a birthday party. I waited until almost noon and began fast stepping it down to the corner. I could see one of them with his hand up in the air waving for me to come on. He was just as excited as I was, but I didn't see the other one. Maybe he is setting up the party for me?"

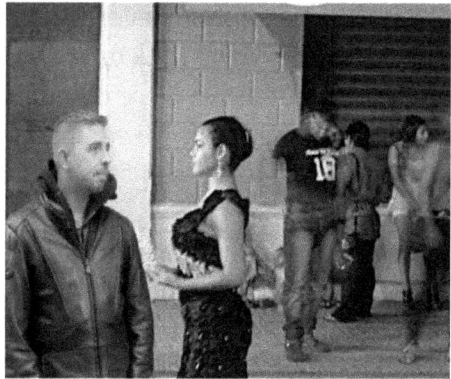

"When we got down to the corner I asked him, 'Where is your friend?'"

"He replied, 'He's in the car, parked around the corner. I set the birthday party up, in the woods like a picnic. Is that okay?'"

"With excitement glowing on our faces and energy building in our stomachs, thoughts danced around in our heads. 'We know older men that are nice-looking, and the other girls don't have this. We are special and today is my birthday. Someone cares enough to throw me a party like a picnic. I just know this is going to be a joyful day.' I could feel the sun on my face and the breeze beginning to blow through my hair as we walked to the car."

"I sat up front with the driver and my girlfriend sat in the backseat with the other man. We were so excited, we begun to giggle and make eye motions at each other. As we was driving down the road we began to make our way to the edge of town. Then the driver turned off onto a little dirt path I have never been down before. I was excited and felt so special. Nobody ever gives me a birthday party, anymore."

Anico's voice took on a darker tone as she continued on with her story. "But as we were driving down the little dirt path the limbs were beginning to thrash against my window. I could see the wind was beginning to pick up as I looked straight up overhead and seen the clouds were black. A big storm was coming. Then the car pulled over and the driver turned himself toward me. The first thought that came to my head was, 'I think he is going to kiss me,' but then he pulled out something from behind his back from under his belt. Then everything went black."

"We were blindfolded and driven somewhere in Romania, to a river. There was a big rubber inflatable boat on the shore, to take us over to Hungary. I had no idea where we were at, but while we were unconscious they dressed us in black clothes. They must had raped us, because I felt sticky down there. I believe they drugged us with something, because I also felt weak and woozy. I could hardly open my mouth except to slur a word. I dozed off again, but could hear the sound of the motor and the sloshing of the waves, hitting the bottom of the boat. I'm guessing we rode for more than an hour or two."

"By the time we made it to the other side of the river it had become to be night. We were told to get out of the boat. I could see as his shirt blew back that one of the men had a gun. The other man had my girlfriend by the arm."

"All four of us began walking through the forest. I could hardly see my hand in front of my face. As we began to walk out from under a group of trees I could see the moonlight shining down on the ground. I tripped over a limb and the man turned to me and said in a quiet voice, 'Be quiet. Don't make no noise. This is the border. If we get caught, we all go to Slovenia prison.'"

"We continued on through the night, using the moon for light. Every time I put my foot down I was feared of getting snake bit or shot by border patrol. Then we came up on what seemed to be a mountain of large rocks cascading into the sky. We began to climb and the man behind me pushed the barrel of his gun in my side, 'Move on. Quicker. Climb on up. You get to the top.'"

"Then, after walking for a good bit of time, we stopped for a second and took a short breather. As we squatted down amongst the bushes, I asked the man, 'Where we headed?'"

"At first, he stalled and didn't say nothing. 'Italy. We're headed Italy.' Then he said, 'Let's go. We need to hurry. It will be daylight shortly. We need to walk faster.' My legs and my feet began to hurt. We began climbing another hill. Once we got at the top I could see the city. We finally arrived into Italy."

"When he got close to the city the man pulled his gun out and put it to my friend's head. In a very rough voice, 'Don't talk or look to no one. I will shoot you and them. Then he put the gun to my head, stood right in front of me and smiled a shit-eating grin."

"We walked and walked down the streets of the city, until my legs began to give out. Then the man grabbed me by the shoulder and pointed at an old condemned looking house. We made our way up the walk to the front door."

"Two more men came out from behind the old house. One of them said, 'Get them in the house now!' We all walked inside. He pulled his gun out from under his belt pointed it toward my stomach. 'Take your clothes off now, before I put a bullet in you or something else.' Then he hit me on the side of my head. Immediately I began to take my clothes off. When I looked over at my girlfriend I could see her clothes dropping to the floor. I felt embarrassed and I could see it on her face, also."

"They began talking in a foreign-language and they continued to talk back and forth. One got angered at the other. He reached into his front pocket. I thought he was gonna pull out a gun, but when he finally removed his hand it was a fistful of money. I had no idea what was going on, but then the man walked over to me and squeezed my butt. Then he walked round to the front of me and put his hands under my breasts, lifting them just a little. Then he reached up and squeezed my jaw to force my mouth open. Then he got down close to me with his eyes and looked at my teeth."

"He shrugged his shoulders and nodded his head, turning back to one of the men that brought us in the house. Then he handed him the money and said something in a foreign language, pointing at our clothes. Then he gestured with his fingers for us to put them back on."

"We walked back outside and were forced to get into a car. My girlfriend was with the other man. I looked out the window, watching. I could see them turn and go down the sidewalk. After that, I never seen her again. After I realized she wasn't coming back I cried more I ever had in my life."

"We began driving and I seen a sign that read 'Rimini'. It was really pretty there. There was lots of water. He pulled into a parking lot of a tall flat condominium next to the water. You could smell the salty air, as the waves crashed upon the rocks."

"We began making our way up the stairs to the third floor and down the hallway. I noticed it was very elegant. He grabbed me by the hair, closing the door behind him and locking it with his key. Then he forced me into one of the bedrooms. It had boarded up windows. He slammed the bedroom door and went to take my clothes off. I started pushing him off of me. He slapped me on the face, then slapped me again, more forcefully. I began to cry, begging, 'Please don't!' as he took off my clothes. He pushed me back on the bed. I went to crawling up toward the head of the bed to get away from him. I could hear his zipper and his pants falling to the floor. As I turned my head to see where he was, he walked to the side of the bed and reached over, grabbed me by the hair and punched me in the stomach, two or three times. I couldn't breathe. I tried to breathe in but couldn't. I could feel his hands on my legs as he begun to part them. I could feel something going in me. I slowly opened my eyes. I could hear him moaning and groaning. My body was sliding toward the headboard so he lifted his body off of me, grabbed my legs, pulled me back to him and went back to having sex with me again. He wouldn't stop."

The girl breaks down and starts weeping on the cot, wrapping her arms around herself, her face buried in the disgusting furniture. Kathy just patted her on the back. "Shhh, not so loud, they might come back..." She looked up at the hole through the ceiling to see if anyone was coming, but apparently they didn't care. Trying to get her to stop crying Kathy asked her to continue.

"This kept going for several hours. I was really sore. I couldn't say anything. I was too scared. Another hour or so I finally just passed out and went to sleep. The next morning I heard the bedroom door unlocking. He come in and pointed me to go to the shower. In a low grumbling voice, he says, 'Go clean your filth for your next client.'"

"I got out of the shower and dried myself off, wrapping myself in a towel. As I stood at the door, I could see a strange man sitting on the side of the bed. He was naked. All his clothes were off and on the floor. He turned and looked at me with a smiling face. He said, 'Come over here and sit with me.' I didn't see where I had a choice as he was more than twice my size. As I walked around to where he was sitting, he reached up and removed the towel that was wrapped around me. He reached up under my arms and slid his hands down the sides of my body. As I was looking down at him, I saw his big hard on. As he went to run his hands back up my body I looked back down at him. His dick was standing straight up. I wasn't used to this."

"He grabbed me and pulled me over onto the bed. As I went to holler and push him off, he put his big hand on my throat and squeezed, choking me. I could not breathe. My face was going to bust. He let up and I coughed and breathed. Coughed and breathed. As fast as lightning, he push my legs up against my chest and begun having sex with me. I was still sore from the last time, but I couldn't stop him from doing it. He kept looking down, watching it go in and pull it out. He stopped and reached over with his hand, grabbed a sheet and wiped off his dick."

"I slowly lifted my head to look across my chest at what he was doing. I seen some blood on the sheets. I wasn't sure if that came out of me or off of him. Then he leaned back over me and continued to have sex. That went on for almost an hour or more. All the sudden he stopped. He was still inside of me. I could feel something starting to get warm in my belly. After a minute passed, he pulled out. I could feel something wet, oozing down between my butt cheeks. He got up, got dressed and walked out the room. Within minutes, another man come in... and he did the same thing."

"This continued on for over two months. Then one day, out of the blue, the pimp walked in the room and said, 'Gather your few things. We're moving.' He turned and left. Then he came back into the room, locking the door behind him."

"He pulled his gun out from under his belt and nodded at

me, waving the gun in the air, as if to remind me who was in charge. We left the hotel and we walked and we walked. Finally, we get to the bus station. I looked up. The sign says this bus is going to Milan, and we board the bus. I remembered that town is near the border of Switzerland, I might be able to make my escape."

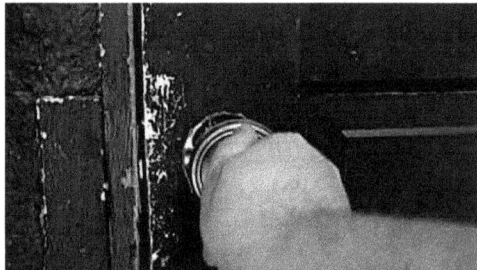

"We rode for hours upon hours. When we arrived in Milan, I could see it was not very big. After we got settled into this dumpy little boardinghouse in the middle of town, he told me he was going to put me on the streets and he will collect the money. I am to walk the client back to the boarding house room and have sex with him. Then I am to clean up and get back to the streets to look for another client."

Chapter 12

"As I was out there on the streets, I didn't see too many of the girls. They weren't out there doing the same thing. This got me thinking, escaping could be easier without them watching me.

"One morning, I got up, getting dressed to go to work, but I began to feel sick. I ran to the little bathroom and threw up. I had already been throwing up for some time, but not like this time. I thought, 'I haven't had my period in way over a month. What if I'm pregnant? There's a big chance I am. I would not want to raise a baby in this environment. He may try to kill the baby. Or maybe he will kill it in order to keep me working on the streets.' The more I thought about it, the more I thought about escaping.

"The next day turned out to be a beautiful spring morning. I could already hear the little birds chirping in the tree outside the room. I guess, no matter where you're at, beauty tries to find its way in.

"Then Fredek said, 'Stop playing sick. You going to make money for me today. Stop getting sick.' Then he turned and went into the bathroom. I was waiting sitting on the side of the bed and I could smell a horrifying smell coming from the bathroom. I heard it flush and when he flung the door open, that smell hit me like a giant dead cow, 'Oow, I cannot wait to go to the streets get out here. Oow! That odor! Nasty.' He was holding his stomach and I could tell by the look on his face that his stomach was churning around and around in pain.

"We made it out to the streets. He would always walk across the street, to where he could keep an eye on me. I had enough freedom to walk up and down the sidewalk so that men could approach me or I could approach them. I was to talk them into having sex with me and give them a price.

"We had been out there for several hours and I hadn't seen nobody. Fredek walked back across the street. He walked up to me and he tried to say something to me, but I don't understand Russian, so he reached down and pulled his shirt back enough to reveal his gun. Then he tapped his chest several times with his finger and pointed to the border house, to the bathroom. Then he gave me that don't-even-think-about-running look. I brushed on a pretty smile. Angry and okay, like everything is gonna be all right.

"He walked off, 'Now might be my only time to escape,' wondering if I'm pregnant or not. When I seen him go in the doorway of the house, I waited a couple seconds, then I ran. I ran and I ran. And when I got to the street corner, I turned and I ran some more.

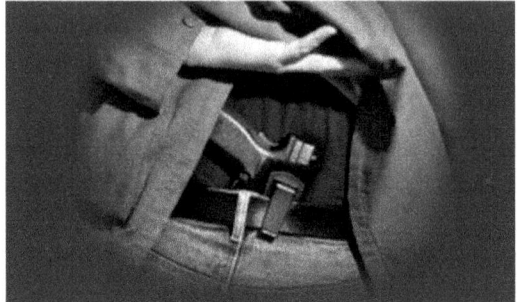

"As I kept running, I could see the big buildings. Then I seen a cop, when I walked over him, he gave me a strange look. Maybe, he was thinking I was going give him a price for sex. As I got closer to him, he finally quit looking at my legs and looked up at my face.

"When I made it to where he was standing, I was panting so hard I collapsed to my knees. I'm sure he could see the sincerity in my eyes, that I had troubles.

"'What's wrong with you, girl? Is somebody chasing you?'

"I raised my head up to look at him, with tears rolling off my cheeks. 'I have been held prisoner and they had been selling me for sex.'

"I think he understood me some, because he motioned for me to get into his car. We walked over to his car and he opened up the back door. I got in. the cop got on his radio and talked for a little while. Then he turned to me. 'Shelter, I take you to. Okay?'

"At this point I didn't care. Any where's gotta be better than where I was. We drove down several streets, then over a block or two. The car started slowing down. He stopped in front of a building, then turned to look back over the seat at me and said, 'Come. She will help you. You're safe here. Get out.

"We got out and walked up to the doorway. When the door opened, a heavyset woman with a long dress said, with a very concerned look on her face, 'Come in.' She had pleasant smile. The officer signaled to me with his hand that he had to go. The Lady reached over and placed her hand on my shoulder. 'My name is Ms. Darlene. Walk with me. I have a room you can stay in until we get you some help.'

"She walked me upstairs and assigned me a room. The lady turned and looked at me again, 'Are you pregnant?'

"'I don't know. Maybe.'

"'I will set you up an appointment with the doctor.' Then she walked off.

"There was a picture on the wall that reminded me of my mom's flower garden. It made me real homesick. 'I live too far from here but I'm close to the border.'

"A couple more days passed and my sickness got worse. I wanted to go home.

"The next day I told the lady what I wanted to do. I told her where I lived and she arranged for a car to take me home. I was really excited, even though I was pregnant. I was still excited about having a baby and raising it on my own.

"The car was getting closer to my mother's house. I was getting very excited as we turned on to the next street. I could see my little brother playing in the street. He was around 12 years old, then.

"When I got out of the car, he looked. He couldn't believe it. That it was me. He run over and hugged me, grabbing me by the arm and pulling me inside the house.

"My mother. She didn't miss me. But I knew this was not true. That night had a big meal and enjoyed our time together. After my brother went to bed, I told my mother what happened.

"Several weeks passed. One night my mother was working late. Me and my brother were sitting on the couch, when we heard a large crash. I turn my head toward the front door and seen it fly open. There he stood in my doorway, the pimp. He was with another guy. He ran over and grabbed me by the hair. The man with him pulled out his knife, reached over and grabbed the lamp, yanking the cord out of the wall. Then, using his knife, he cut the cord and handed it to the pimp. Then he pulled my arms behind me and tied them with the lamp cord. I swung my head around to check on my brother. The other man was holding him down, by the throat.

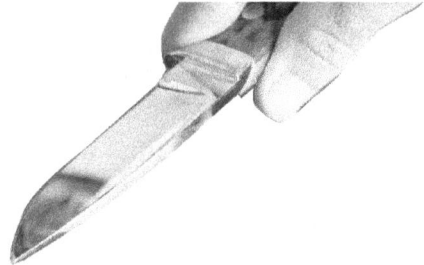

"Then our dog jumped up on the man holding my brother. He barked and bit him on the leg. I continued to watch. Then the pimp that tied me, walked over to the other guy, grabbed his knife and stuck it into my dog.

"'Benji! My dog!' I began to yell. Then he just laid over on the floor and didn't move anymore. The man holding my little brother, unzipped my brother's pants while the pimp pulled them off of him. They took him to the couch and turned him over, raping him. My little brother hollered, as I tried to make my way over to him. The other guy slapped me in the face, knocking me backwards. He walked over to me and said, 'This is what you get for telling the police about me. I told you, I know where you live.'

"After they was through with my little brother, they took the other lamp and pulled from the wall, using his knife to cut the cord loose from the lamp. He tied my little brother's arms up behind his back, pulling his ankles up and tying them together. He reached down to the floor and picked up my little brother's sock and pushed it into his mouth. They grabbed me by my hair and arm, pulling me out the back door of the house and across the field to the other street, where a van was waiting.

"They pushed me into the back of the van and drove off down the road. I was tied up and left laying in the back. The pimp turned around to look at me, "Your friend. Your friend that was taken with you. She is dead now.'

"'What happened to her?'

"'She would not do what they asked. The men that had her in Israel, they gave her some drugs. She still would not do her job, so they threw her off a six story building.'

"When we finally got where we were going, the van pulled around to the back of a house. The two men jumped out and opened the side door of the van. Reaching in, they grabbed me by the arm and walked me into the back door of the house. A man was standing there. He looked like a doctor. 'Bring her into my examination room.'

"When the doctor walked through the doorway, he gestured with his hands, 'Put her up on the table.' I was laying there, shivering due to how cold the table was. I was scared. I felt it best to just to shut my eyes. I felt something on my face. When I opened up my eyes, the doctor was holding a mask over my nose and mouth. I started getting dizzy and passed out.

"When I came to, my ankles were handcuffed to the bed, I was lying in. I started coming back to all my senses. My eyes wandered around the room, looking for anything that would tell me what's going on. That's when I started to lift up and rollover. I still had the baby. I'm not sure what the doctor did.

"I did whatever they told me to do. I did not want to bring more harm on to my family, so I continued to work for them for quite a few years in order to protect them. Over the next few months the baby continued to show more. I was getting bigger. They allowed me to have the baby. Only thing that come to my mind, 'That's one more person I will need to protect. I'll do that by doing whatever I'm told.'

"The baby was born. A baby girl. I named her Jozsa. She was so beautiful. One day I told the pimp, 'I want my daughter to go live with my mother.'

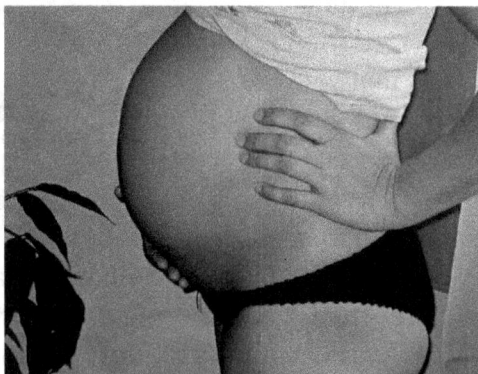

"He agreed, 'Tomorrow I will have someone take her there.'

"I took a piece of paper and wrote, 'Please let my daughter live at your sister's house, in Sweden, so she will be safe.' Then I wrapped it in plastic and put it down in her diaper.

"A couple weeks passed and we boarded a bus for Turkey. It seemed strange though. Even after everything that had happened, they began to give me more freedom. I could walk to the store and buy myself a bag of chips or a Pepsi, without them watching me. They even allowed me to start working the nightclubs in Turkey. This was much safer than working the streets.

"After being there several months, he decided that we were going to move to London. He had already called ahead and talk to a guy who owns a brothel there. The man from London told him how to smuggle me in.

"Once we got there and got settled in, the client would make his way back to my room at the brothel. I would sometimes ask the men for money, but they would reply, No, I cannot give you money.'

"I would try to explain to them, 'I just want to go home. I have a new daughter.' I'd look up at their face. They didn't care. They only cared about having sex with me.

"Most of the time the clients were so drunk, they didn't care about what I wanted. They would say what they wanted me to do for them, or should I say to them. But they were not there for me to talk to. I had nobody to talk to or to help me. At times they would ask me, 'Why are you here if you don't like your job? I would just shrug my shoulders. If I told them they might tell my pimp what I said. I knew they weren't going to help me anyhow.

"I got a chance to get out of the room, from time to time. I could see some of the other girls, but we never talk to one another. Most of them were Eastern European. None of them were British at all. One of the other girls could de-friend you in order to make a little money or drugs from the pimp. It was too dangerous to talk to anybody. The girls. The clients. All due to the fear of the pimps. All the girls here had pimps. The pimps pay to rent the room at the brothel. Sometimes, as I'm lying there in bed, I would look up. I saw a microphone on the ceiling and another one behind the air-conditioner fan. I spent a lot of time in that room. Weeks upon weeks. Never going outside the door.

"One day at the brothel in North West London, the door flew open. It was a police officer. We were being raided. The

police officer said, 'Come with me,' and I went out the door. A lady cop walked me to a police van. They loaded up all the girls in one van. I was looking out the little port window of the van and seen they were putting the guys who ran the place and some of the pimps into police cars. Then we all headed downtown. It was just like going on a class field trip.

"When we got down to the police station, they took me into a room for questioning. They asked me for names, 'Who is running this operation?' They were asking me if I know certain names. I listened to them making their best deal. Their best offer for me to give up some names, 'We can protect you. You're safe with us.' But I knew better. 'Blah, blah, blah, I ain't telling you shit' I knew my family would be in danger. I was not going to take a risk after everything I've been through. My family, too.

"I was sitting in my cell, thinking about the police. 'They don't know what they're up against. What I'm up against. The system, circle that I have been snared into. It's much bigger than just one little police station. Always traffickers, they work together like brotherhood. Occasionally somebody tries to come in and take over, but they are short-lived.'

"During the time of my incarceration, my boss, I should say my pimp, came and visited me a few times. He walked right up into the police station, to check on me. To intimidate me, so I would stay quiet. The police finally started putting it together. And I got hopeful, thinking 'Somebody just might say something. I don't know. They know I was trafficked.' But then the immigration officers showed up and decided to move me back to Moldova. Immigration knew there was no real risk, no safety problem if they release me. The only place I had to go was back to my mother's house where she and my brother live.

"A week later as I was walking to the store. A car drove up next to me and the back door flew open. Somebody grabbed me from behind and pulled me into the car, as fast as you could get bitten by a snake. I could hear the door slam close. 'The traffickers found me again.'

"They drove me just outside of town, down a little gravel road, into a wooded area and pulled me out of the car. They beat me until I could not move. Then all three of them took turns, raping me, doing whatever they thought would hurt the most. Somebody reached down and helped me stand up. Out of the corner of my eye, the one not swollen, I could see one of them making a noose out of a rope. He slid it on my neck. One of the other guys had a shovel. He dropped it at my feet and hollered out with a deep voice, 'Start digging your grave, Bitch.'

Chapter 13

"I looked at the shovel. All of this is very familiar. I have been through this before. I just knew that as soon as I dug the hole, they would drag me back to the car and take off. So I reached down, the noose still hanging off my neck. I picked up the shovel and started digging. The ground was real soft. I kept digging. Then somebody come up behind me and put their arms around my waist, lifting me up in the air a few feet."

"As the man lowered me, I could feel the rope tightening. I looked around using the only eye I could see out of. One of the other men was tying a rope around the tree limb, just above my head. After he got it tied, he let go of my waist. My feet were still on the ground, but the limb was pulling the rope up, tightening around my neck. I couldn't breathe. I was getting dizzy. My knees got wobbly. I was fixin' to pass out. I just knew I was fixin' to die. It didn't matter to me. I began to fall. I heard a tree limb snap."

"When I came to I seen laying across the ground a saw next to the end of the limb. Someone was loosening the rope around my neck, pulling it over my head. Somebody else grabbed me by my ankles and pulled me. The two of them picked me up and put me in the truck of their car. By this point I was so tired of crying. I was tired of living. Dying would be a good favor for me."

"I could hear the car cranking up then it spun down the gravel road. After a short while I could hear the tires screeching against the pavement as he turned on to the blacktop road. We drove for several hours. Then the car slowed down and we drove for another twenty or thirty minutes. Then I could feel the car idling at a slow speed as we pulled up into the driveway. He shut the motor off, opened up the trunk and they grabbed me. One grabbed me by my ankles and the other one grabbed me under my arms."

"They took me in the house and laid me on the living room floor. It was a room full of men. They were very intoxicated and had been drinking for some time. They started discussing who was going to get me first. Then somebody hollered out in a deep voice, 'I paid the most. I should go first.' Mocking them, 'All the rest of y'all, you can get sloppy seconds; and thirds and fourths and fifths.' He paused for a second, 'Well damn. Just how many we got over here, anyhow?'"

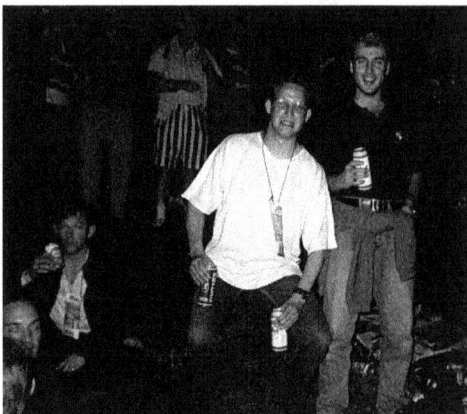

"Somebody in the back hollered out, '27 men.'"

"'Girl you're gonna be busy all night.' They began raping me, being as brutal as they could imagine."

"After several hours had passed one of the main traffickers told the man, 'You have to stop doing that. Pull that bottle out of her! I've got a connection to sell her to an Israeli trafficker.' I just laid there, unable to move. I was sore in places I didn't know I had. They worked me over good. At least then I understood why they were keeping me alive. So I could be sold again. I still didn't look too bad. All my scars were inside. Anybody paying for sex would never see my scars."

"I believe I had just turned 26. Of course I was trying to forget my birthday. Can you believe it? Being gang raped on your birthday? How fucked up life is..." She gave a jaded scoff before continuing. "I was trying to ignore life, what little bit of it I was able to see, or what they allowed me to see. Somebody helped me back to the car. The trunk of the car. We drove for a little ways, making it to another house. They walked me in and put me into a bedroom. The windows were all boarded up and a dirty mattress was laying on the floor. There was a peapod in the other corner of the room. I rested there for a couple days. They fed me and walked me to the shower to clean me up."

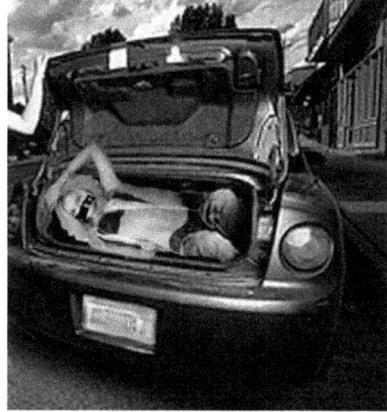

"Then that afternoon, I could hear the jingle of keys as they unlocked the door. My boss, soon-to-be-ex-boss or pimp, was handing me some new clothes. I can't even remember the last time I had new clothes. Even at home, living with my mom. He came at me holding a syringe. I could see just past him in the living room a big box, with an address label on the side. 'He's gonna put me to sleep, stick me in that box and put me on a plane headed to Tel Aviv, Israel.' By the time I worked it out in my head, I felt the pinch of the needle, 'At least they fed me good.' was the last thought through my head as I quickly dozed off into a deep, deep sleep.'

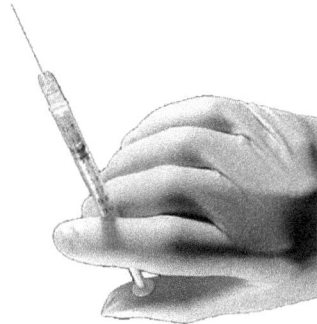

Raising her head back up a bit Amunet looked to Kathy with a pitiful look in her eyes. "Then I woke up here. I've never been to one of these auctions. That's what's going on here, right?"

Kathy said, "I do believe so. I will look. I need to get up and stretch my legs anyway. Thanks for telling me your story. Maybe I'll see you later."

Kathy walks away, recalling her time with the girl she just left. "She seems more relaxed, after telling me her story." The girls' stories are running through her head, tales of horrific abuse and exploitation making her own stomach nervous. She knows that this soon will be her life if she can't escape. She walks across the room, feeling good for being able to talk to somebody, but their stories are horrifying and so similar to hers.

Kathy sees another girl sitting in a chair, with an empty one next to her. Thinking she would like to sit down for a little while she made her way over and placed her hand on the girl's shoulder. "Hey, my name is Kathy. What is yours?"

She looks up, her mascara and blush messed from her tears. "I'm Laura."

When Kathy looks back at her, I notices she is a very pretty girl. She has short hair cut off below her ears, a Dutch boy haircut, large green eyes, and a model's face. She was filled out, with nice size breasts for girl of her age. She looks to be about nineteen years old. Long slender legs. "How did you manage to get here?"

Laura let's go of a breath she didn't know she had been holding, then sighs. "Well, I was going to college in Georgia. I had a night class I was attending. The professor asked me to wait after class; he needed to talk to me about improving my grade. We had just taken a test and was going over them. He stood up and asked me to walk to the front of the class room. Everybody else had done departed from the room. I walked up to his desk and he walked round to meet me, 'I can show you how to make a higher score, but we all need to benefit, right?'"

"I guess that was his hint: Sex in exchange for a passing grade in psychology. It would change my life. I lifted up my head and looked him in the eyes, 'I'll do whatever I need to do. Whatever it takes to pass this course, Mr. Gilbert.'"

"The teacher reached up and grabbed me by the shoulders, leaning me over his desk. He fucked me for seems like an hour. I kept telling myself 'Whatever it takes to get a good grade. Whatever it takes to get a good grade!'"

"I decided to just go ahead and close my eyes. All of the sudden I felt a cloth over my nose and mouth. He was bearing down on me. It had a strange odor to it. It was burning my sinuses. My eyes began to get hazy and tears began to run down my face."

"After that I don't remember anything, until I woke up in a darkroom. I began to cry. I was so scared. The fear of not knowing what was going to happen next. The sex itself didn't scare me. My dad had been raping me since I was a young girl, around the age of ten years old."

"But I was scared of dying and being cut up, selling my body parts." She looks up to Kathy with disdain written all over her face. "You know this happens a lot in foreign countries. There's a big market on the internet for buying body parts and there're never any questions asked. Were they come from. Not when it comes to saving somebody's life. Someone that's fighting for their own life."

"I heard the door unlocking. Two men were standing in the doorway. One of them was holding a syringe. I pushed myself back into the corner of the small room. One of them grabbed my leg and yanked me back to them. I felt the needle going in. Then I passed out."

"I believe I rode in a secret compartment on an eighteen wheeler, wearing a blindfold and a gag the whole time." She stopped telling her story, and looked over at Kathy. "What is your name? And how did you get here?"

Kathy tried to give her a smile, but she wasn't sure if she could muster one due to the situation. "I'm Kathy. My dentist was working on my teeth and offered to give me a ride home. He put a rag over my face and I passed out. Then I rode in a plane for a long ways and woke up here. I did hear one of them talking to the other about an auction here in Mexico City."

Getting up from the chair Laura said, "I've got to go the bathroom. I'll be back. Maybe we can talk some more." Kathy watched her walk across the dimly lit room to the corner where the piss can was, all the way until she crouched over it. Turning her eyes away she notices a girl across the room. When she stands up she looks to be five foot tall. She has a dark tan and beautiful blue eyes. Dark brown hair running down past her shoulders with streaks of blonde hair. Very slender built. Kathy gets up and walks over to where the girl and sits down next to her. She is very young. Maybe fourteen years old, hard to tell. She is panicking. She turns to her, "Hi my name is Kathy. What's yours? And how did you get here?"

"Susan. My name is Susan." The young girl doesn't even look at Kathy, instead she focuses on her hands, her fingers shaking as they fumble over one another. "I was taking a night course at a vo-tech school for business. I was unlocking my car and a man came up from behind me. He put his hand on my throat and held a gun to the side of my face and said, 'Don't move and don't scream or it will be your last.' I heard a van door sliding open. Another hand came around to my face and put a black cover over my head, grabbing me and pulling me back into the van. As I laid there, begging to let me go, one of the men tied a gag around my mouth and tied my arms behind my back. Then I heard the van cranking up and driving off. Seems like we drove for miles. Miles and miles before we finally stopped.

"I could hear the door sliding open as somebody reached down under my arm, saying 'Get up. Get up, now!' We began to walk. It must've still been dark because I could smell the night air. We stopped for a minute and I could hear the jingling of keys. Then I heard the click of something unlocking and we start walking again. I could see some light coming through the black hood on my head, but no images or shadows. We walked into another room. It was dark. Then, all the sudden, he pushed me down. I fell on something soft, a mattress, and he said 'Don't move. Stay here.' I was too scared to move. I laid there for a long time, crying and shaking, not knowing if I may get out of this alive or not. Then I could hear the door opening up again."

"A light turned on; I still had the black hood over my head and my hands were still bound together. I felt the mattress move. Somebody was kneeling on it. Then I felt something; a knife on my throat."

"He said, 'Don't move, girl! I need to check you out.' I could feel his hand on my hip as he rolled me over onto my back. I could feel him unsnapping my pants and unzipping them. I began to get really scared, not knowing what he would do to me. I'd heard so many horror stories about things that can happen to girls. Someone sticking a big object up in them. Or even dry pumped in the ass. I tried to beg, but nothing would come out because of how tight the gag was in my mouth. All I could do was moan and that was not stopping him."

"He grabbed my back pockets to get my pants off. I could feel the bed move as he knelt down on it. Then I felt the rest of my pants sliding off my legs. Chills ran through my body. I was petrified. Too scared to move. I continue thinking about that knife. What he might do to me. He might even stick the knife up in my vagina. I could feel his hands on my hips as he pulled my panties down to my knees and then off my legs. I started feeling butterflies in my stomach. I got to thinking, 'If I throw up with this gag on I drown in my own vomit.' He reached up with his hands, grabbing me under my knees and pushing my legs back toward my chest. I felt something wet down there. It was his finger. He had spit on it. I began to feel sick. I thought I was going to throw up. It felt like there was hundreds of butterflies in my stomach. Then I felt something different, but wet."

Chapter 14

Laura was crying again, tears streaming down her face. Kathy does as she did with the other girls, rubbing Laura's back to try and console her. "Only thing to come to mind is he was sticking his tongue and licking me. I begun to gag. I was scared to throw up, as it would stay in my mouth. I heard him say, 'Come on down girl. You're overreacting. And you're not gonna stop me anyhow. If I wanna fuck that thing I will.' I heard his zipper as something fell to the floor. I'm sure it was his pants dropping."

"I could feel the bed moving again as he got back on. He pushed my knees back up against my chest. I could feel something against my vagina, it was hard but soft. All I could think was, 'Please, go easy and not try to hurt me and please don't kill me afterwards. I just have to survive and try to stay alive.' He raped me for at least two hours straight. Then he rolled me over."

"I could feel his big, gross hands on my butt, pulling my cheeks apart. I could feel his hand reaching down underneath and wiping my vagina from where he came in me, smearing it up on my booty. Then I could feel something big pushing against me. It was beginning to go in my butt. Oh God, it hurts so badly. I could feel him pulling it out. It seemed like the pain wouldn't stop throbbing, then he pushed it in again. This time even deeper. I could feel it going up into my stomach. I thought I was going to throw up again. I hollered, but with the gag in my mouth it was no louder than a loud moan. I had never felt pain like this before."

"The butterflies in my stomach had turned into bees. It was hurting. I had never felt pain like that before. And I was still scared for my life. I kept thinking, 'Am I going to get out of this alive?'"

"Three days later, I was really beginning to stink from his cum and his sweaty body being on me. I could hear the door unlocking, then I could feel his hand under me lifting me up and saying, 'It's bath time.' He kept the black hood on me the whole time. 'I need you to wash up real good. You better wash that pussy on the inside and out. I'm going to let your hands go, but do not take off that hood. I'm going to help you step into the tub. I will hand you the soap and washcloth. If you're good I will feed you another sandwich.'"

"After I had completely washed up I heard him unlocking the door and his footsteps coming in. He grabbed me by the arms, slapping me, saying, 'Stand up!' He handed me a towel and told me to dry off as he stood there watching me. I couldn't cry anymore. I had done cried out all I could do. At this point I wasn't sure if I wanted to live or die. Not that I even had a choice. After I dried off he handed me some clothes. They felt like mine but I wasn't sure. After I got dress, he said, "Put your hands behind your back. He tied me up again and we started walking. 'I don't think we're headed back to the room where I came from. I think we're going in the other direction. I heard the door locking and the knob turning.

"He pulled me through the door. I could feel the fresh air. I heard a clicking sound; a gun being cocked. My knees began to bow and as I started to go down he grabbed me. My leg rubbed up against a car. The next thing came to my mind was he was putting me in the trunk of the car. As we were standing there I could feel the bumper up against my knees. He said, 'Get in.' and he pushed me down into the trunk with his hand on top my head. He said, "Lie down and stay still. If you're good I'll get you a hamburger and Coke. I could hear the trunk slamming. It seemed like I laid there forever. I heard two car doors closed. They cranked up and I heard another humming sound. I think it was a carport door raising up or something."

"I felt the car move, as my body jerked to one side. We was on the road for hours. Once or twice I doze off. I'd wake up thinking, 'They're going to kill me. He hadn't gotten me the hamburger and Coke that he promised.' I could feel the car coming to a stop. I thought they were fixing to let me out, but then the car started rolling again. It picked up speed and there was a rumbling noise in the trunk. It lasted for hours while we were driving.

"Many hours later they stopped the car. I heard them pop the trunk open. He took the gag off my mouth and lifted the black hood just up to my nose. 'Open your mouth.' I felt something pushing up against my lips. It was a straw. I begun sucking. I didn't want stop. He pulled it away from me."

"'Slow down, girl. You're drinking too fast. Now put your mouth here on some hamburger. Open a little bit bigger.' I could smell the hamburger as he held it up to my lips. It tasted so good. I could've eaten ten of them."

"After I finished my drink and ate the last of the hamburger he pulled the bag back down over my head. As he was trying to put the gag back in my mouth 'Hey Mister. I've gotta go to the bathroom.'"

"'Soon. Lay down.' And he slammed the trunk. The car cranked up and we were going again. I was trying not to pee, but some of it oozed out. By that point I just couldn't hold it any longer and I began to spray myself. Soaking myself as it ran down my leg and onto my back pockets. After five or six minutes, I began to get cold from where I had peed myself and my stomach started cramping up from my bowels, but I was able to hold it more easily."

"Several hours later, the car finally stopped. I could hear people walking around. They were speaking in Spanish, which I don't speak. The car started up again. We rode for another hour or two. Then I could hear we were on gravel. All the sudden I could smell the dust as it was finding its way into the trunk and I could hear the car coming to a stop.

"I laid there for another good twenty minutes or so before the trunk lid finally popped open. Someone reached up under my arms and began pulling me out of the trunk. I could feel my legs cramping from having laid in one spot for so long. Then someone said, 'See. She has peed on herself. Get her on down into the room.'"

"We started walking down some steps. He had a gag on me, but he pulled the bag off my head and untied my arms as he shoved me into this room. I've been in here for days."

"I have no idea where we are. I'm guessing we're not in the United States anymore. That's all I can come up with. I don't know why or what is gonna happen to us." Then she began to whimper and cry again.

Not knowing what else to do for her Kathy just pats her on the back. Then Kathy sees a very nice-looking, light-colored Spanish girl with satin-like hair. She turns and looks at Kathy as she walks towards her. She has light brown eyes and was sitting in the far corner of the room. As Kathy gets near her the girl doesn't acknowledge her at first. She seemed out of it. Kathy places her hand on the girl's shoulder and says, "Do you mind if I sit down with you. I need someone to talk to and it seems we could both use a new friend, right? What is your name?"

With a stuttering voice of fear the girl responds, "S-Sophia. That's my name."

"How did you end up get here?

"My uncle. My uncle sold me. He has been raping me for years. Now that my little sister is older he figured he could sell me off since they needed money. They paid him fifteen hundred for me. There's not much work in the town where we live. And my family is very poor. The garden doesn't produce too good and when you get hungry you have to do anything you can to stay alive. You would do anything to keep your kids from being hungry. You do what you have to do. That's where I come from. There's not too many choices. As I see it, at least here I will get something to eat. At least here I may get some new clothes or shoes. I just wish there was a way I could send some money back to my family."

Kathy didn't like the way the girl seemed to be justifying her uncle selling her into this terrible life. Her eyes narrowed as she wonders just what could make Sophia think this was better than where she came from. That it was okay she was being tricked out by these awful people.

"But like I heard you as you was telling that girl I don't know what's going to happen. I don't know the outcome. Or even if in the end we will live or die. Where I'm from you hear about girls and young women being sold to human traffickers. If you're pretty and your body is built to their liking they will pay good money. This kind of business has been around for more than a thousand years."

"For some women, they go off to live in another country that's wealthier to live and work for good people. Keep your house clean. Work in your garden. Take care of your farm animals. Some girls may be happier here than in their own home. It's a flip of the coin. Some end up in a brothel serving a man's needs day and night; but there're all kinds of brothels, and all kinds of owners. Each one is run a little differently. At a high end brothel one your clients may say to the owner, 'I want to buy that girl,' and your owner has a right to sell you, and you have to hope that your new owner has good intentions for you."

"Other girls may work in massage parlors, bars, or strip clubs; and even saunas and spas, doing whatever the boss tells them to do."

Bundesarchiv, Bild 101II-MW-1019-07

"Some women think having to lay on your back ten to twelve hours a day, having sex with men is the worst there is; but I got news for you. It's not. There are always worse situations to be in. One is being sold to somebody who puts you in bondage. You become their slave. They'll repeatedly put pain on you every day for many years."

"Another place you don't want to end up in is the human meat market. If you end up there, they'll cut you into pieces and sell the parts to hospitals and clinics around the world. A young attractive woman will bring a higher price than anything else on earth. She can be used, over and over by the same person to make money and anything else. For as long as a man gets a hard on a woman will always be needed."

"So as you can see, our two worlds are so far apart that we think totally differently, but yet our two worlds are the same."

Kathy says, "You seem to know a lot about this. I know if we're both strong, we can get through this together. I think I'm going to go back over there and sit down. I need to try to get me some rest." Kathy walks back over to where she had been sitting and notices another girl looking up at her. She has a very scared look on her face. Kathy can tell that she has been crying for some time.

The girl asks her in a quiet and demure voice, "Can I talk to you?"

"Yes. My name is Kathy. What's yours?"

"Angelique."

"Where you from, Angelique?"

"Brazil."

"How did you manage to get here?"

She looks back down at the floor and sadly replies, "There was a lady that came to our town. She knocked on my family's door, claiming she was a counselor with the family planning office. She said if I worked with her she would show me how to set up my own business, saying that she has several people now working with her that are starting their own businesses. She came over and made visits to me and my mother throughout the week. We came to be friends. Or so I thought."

"One night my mom invited her to stay and eat supper with us. She told my parents about all of the successful people she helped get started with their own business. She went on to say that with just a little bit of schooling it wouldn't be long before I'd be working for myself. Maybe I'd also be hiring some of my friends to work for me, too. Then she added this is how she got started. A counselor came to her little town and worked with her until she learned how to run her own business and council others to do the same. She said this is something she had always wanted to do. To help others become independent so that they can own their own lives and never have to be a slave to the world."

Chapter 15

"She showed us pamphlets filled with lots of pictures of different businesses and asked me what kind of business I would like to go into? And where I'd like it to be?

"I told the counselor, "Probably here, where I'm living. And, I would like to go in the counseling. I'd love to help others start their businesses, if that's possible?

"The woman told me, "Yes. I move around. I don't stay in one town. A couple of weeks from now, I'll be in a whole new country. That's what you can do, too. You could work from here, but then go visit other countries. Then you could come back.

"Then she continued, 'Maybe after I visit with you a couple of more times, you can give me a list of some of your friends, so that I can call them. Make sure they're fairly attractive. After that, we can go out, door to door. Or, if it's okay with your parents, you can fly with me to another country and get paid for helping me to show others how they can get started in a business.'

"After a week went by, I gave her a list of some of my nicest looking friends. One's I thought she would be interested in talking to. When she contacted my friends later, they said they would come back to her. They were very excited about the opportunity of starting their own businesses and excited that she was gonna take them out and teach them, also. As my dad and mom began to trust her, they began to leave her alone in the room with me.

"She said, 'How about tomorrow morning. I will stop by here and we will walk through the neighborhood and find us some doors to knock on. It will be just like my first time an you will be so excited.'

"The next day, I did my best to dress up like a businesswoman. Looking in the mirror, I felt so good about myself. I knew I would be able to help my parents with their money problems. And even teach my little sister how to run a business when she gets older, too. 'My life is fixing to make a change. People will look up to me. I know I'll feel good about myself, helping others to do things they want to.'

"When she arrived we headed out the door. I turned to tell mom-mom and paw-paw that I would see them later that afternoon. I'm sure I had to been high-stepping it out to the street. I was not used to high heels. They were so pretty. Dark blue with little sparkles in them when the sun hit them.

"We walked down the street. She said, "Let's turn down that street and find a door to knock on. As soon as we turned onto the street, I noticed a van parked near the sidewalk. I had never seen that van before in our neighborhood. But I felt safe because things couldn't be much better right then. I don't think I'd ever felt more on-top-of-the-world than at that moment. Even had a big thunder shower come down on me, I wouldn't had felt bad. I knew this lady was going to help me get my life going.

"Then as we got close to the van, the lady walked so that I was between her and the vehicle. I heard the van door slide open and all of the sudden, I felt someone pushing me by my shoulders. I could not run because of my shoes. Then I lost my balance and somebody grabbed me under my arms and pulled me into the van, putting their hands over my mouth.

"I was screaming and looking around. I saw the lady as she closed the sliding door and got into the front seat, to drive the van. She took off very fast and in no time, she had made it to the edge of town. She handed me a bottle of water and said, "Drink it. Drink it now.' Shortly after that I passed out. I don't know for how long.

"When I woke up, I could not move my hands, as they had been tied behind my back. Everything was dark, but I could hear traffic. I could not see them. Being scared, I began to holler, but I could not holler out loud because something was in my mouth.

"I heard her say, 'Just lay still. You're going to be okay. We don't want to hurt you. Just lay still.' I began to cry. I had never been a part of anything like this. I had always been cared for by my parents. They had always watched over me. Protected me. There was no way I could've imagined this ever happening to me.

"I began to feel that we were getting far from my house. As time played on, I could hear the road sounds changing from hard road to a gravel road. Then the van started slowing down and finally came to a stop. When I woke up again, I heard the side door slide open. Someone reached in, grabbed me from under the arms and pulled me out of the van. I felt something covering my head. A thin cloth sack. As they lifted me up, I could feel the sun on my face and then shortly after that, I could not.

"I heard a heavy door slamming. It smelled musky, like an old building or barn. Somebody pick me up completely into the air and then laid me down, lifting my head back up and pulling off the gag. He told me to drink. It tasted like the other water did, I knew then that I would probably be going back to sleep. They put the gag back in my mouth and laid my head back down. I heard something sliding over my head. Then I heard hammering. It was echoing. I wanted to roll around, but I could feel the sides. 'I really believe I'm in a big box. It smells like old wood.' I dozed off again.

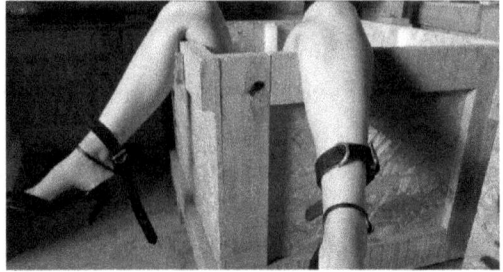

"The next time I woke up, I could hear something clacking. Metal against metal. I heard an air horn. I sounded like it might've been a train. Yep, I think I was riding on a train, but I passed back out. The next time I woke up, I was here and I was laying down on that bed, over there." As she points to the far end of the room.

Kathy stands up and hears the door unlocking. The sound of it echoes through the room. Most of the girls turn their heads, hoping to be released. Two men walk in. They have a long chain with several belts hooked to it. The first guy says, "Okay girls. Stand up and face the wall. Take all of your clothes off. Its shower time." One of the men took the end of the chain and walked to the girl furthest away and put the belt around her waist. Then he locked it, with a small pad lock.

Kathy pulls her clothes off and sees the man working his way toward her. He puts the belt around her waist. Kathy can feel knots in her stomach. Her legs are shaking so much. She feels her knees are going to collapse.

The guy works his way through the girls, locking each of their belts. Then he backs off to the corner of the room. The other guy, near the door says, "Come on, ladies. Shower time. Let's go."

They march like soldiers up the stairs and around the corner to another big room which is set up as a big shower room. He says, "Come on. Let's get cleaned up." Then he turns the water on and gets the soap from off of the table.

They clean themselves up, making themselves feel just a little bit better about life but. Not much, but sometimes just a good shower helps. Kathy turns around and notices that the girls giggling now, just like a physical education shower back in high school. Of course, most of these girls look like they're right out of high school and most of them look like they could be models. As they continue their shower, the man stands at the door, watching them. Kathy kept thinking, "He may decide to come in here and raped one of us. He has that look on his face"

All of the sudden, the man pulls his knife out of his scalber and drops his pants. As he does, the other man comes up to the door and watches. Kathy keeps washing herself, hoping that if she ignores what's going on, she'll be safe.

The man walks down to the girl at the far end and starts with her. He says, "Turn around. Put your hands on the wall and step back. Step back. Straddle your feet apart to get under the water. Let it run down your back." Then he grabbed her around her waist, pulling her back, while taking the hand (holding the knife) and shoving on her back, forcing her to push her ass outward. Then he slid his dick between her legs. All she can do is stand there. The other girls hear her cry out in pain.

After what seems like ten minutes, he backs up from her and says, "You're clean." Stepping over to the next girl, Kathy realizes he's making his way toward her.

The man grabs the girl from underneath with one hand, and with his other hand, he pushes her back downward, pulling her butt back toward him. He strokes her back and forth. She screamed from the pain, which was more than she could bare.

At this point, Kathy looks over her shoulder, "I'm not feeling all that safe. Whatever is happening to her I'm sure will happen to me."

He pulled himself out of her, "She's clean." Then hollered, "Next!" It echoed through the room.

Kathy turns her head to look at the man by the door. A smiling grin is playing upon his lips.

The guy continues until only Kathy is left as she is the one nearest the door, "I want to run." Her body is flinching from nerves. Her feet slip out from under her when the chain tightens up.

I felt a hand on my head. He reaches over and grabbed Kathy by the hair, pulling her head straight up into the air, pushing Kathy under the shower nozzle. "You want to run, huh, little one? Ha, let me give you something to run from"

Then he hollered out, "All you girls, need to get use to dick. For most of you, if not all of you, the dick will be a big part of your life. You want to serve it. If you serve it well, you will live well. If you do not serve it well, then you won't live well or for long."

Kathy feels his hand sliding under her waist and pulling her back, while his hand with the knife shoves down on her back. The water continues to run off her head and down her back. Kathy feels him putting his dick between her legs, rubbing her womb as he pushes himself up in her. "He's tearing me open. It's going into my stomach. It hurts," Kathy thinks to herself. He kept this up for several minutes. "The pain is letting up some. I'm more feared for my life, than feared of the pain." He pulls out and rubs it up the crack of her butt, "I am so scared. This is what the other girls were screaming about." Kathy felt a new pain like she'd never felt before. "He is starting to push it in my anal. He is working on me harder than he did the others. It feels like he is tearing my insides out. He just keeps pushing it up further. I swear, he is bumping my stomach." As Kathy looks straight down, she tries to put this terrible moment out of my mind. She begins to see blood going down her leg. As it makes it to her knee, the water washes it off. "I don't think this moment will ever end and yet he moans like he's having a good time."

The guy stops, completely emerged in Kathy. She feels something warm inside her. "I can't figure.' He continued to stay steadily holding his dick completely emerged in me, "Oh, he's cumming in me. He's cumming in my ass."

Then he begins slowly pulling it out, handing Kathy the washcloth. "Well, shove it down there. Wash it up down there, real good. Push that washcloth up in that ass. Let me see you do it. If you don't, I will. I will wrap it around my dick and slide it up in there. Keep, keep rubbing it clean."

Then he commands all the girls, "Wash out one more time and turn the water off. We need to go." He grabs an armload of towels and starts handing them out to each one of them saying, "Dry off. Get that hair dry. Dry them legs. Them arms. And them cute booties."

Then he got dressed. "Come on. Follow me into the next room. You've all got to get dressed."

They're all standing there, shivering, in one room. Kathy turns to Angelique "It's kinda cold in here."

The other man comes back into the room, carrying two large totes. He sets the totes on the floor and removes their tops. Kathy looks at them. They were both filled with bikini swimwear and a large assortment of brightly colored lingerie. Some of them shined from the light. The man walks over to the first girl and pops her on top of her head, "Reach in and get something. Get dressed." Then he gestures to the others, "That goes for all of you. Now!" Then he chuckles, "You don't want me to dress you. If I do it, you will get some more of that same treatment, I gave you in the shower. But, far rougher. I like it when it's rough."

"First; I want you to lineup. Right here. Single row. All of you. Open your mouth. Take this pill. It will help you to relax."

Then the other man stands in front of the first girl, "Open your mouth."

Kathy turns her head to see what's going on to see the man placing a pill into the next girl's mouth, "Move your tongue. All right. Next. Take this pill. Let me see in your mouth."

As he gets to Kathy, she opens her mouth and closes her eyes. She can feel his fingers dropping the pills onto her tongue. As she swallows the pill, she squints her eyes because the bitter taste makes her cringe.

When Kathy finally reopens her eyes, he had already handed us all pills.

After about twenty minutes, Kathy says to Laura "I am feeling more relaxed and feeling a little sexier, too."

Kathy looks around I notices the other girls are feeling the same thing. They begin dancing around, having forgotten where they are. Partying like, they'd totally forgotten what had just happened to them in the shower and not knowing what's in store for their future.

But after the stories Kathy had heard from the other girls, they're not gonna get much of a future. Not the way they are living, anyhow.

Chapter 16

The man walks back into the room, "C'mon. Finish getting dressed, Ladies."

They all reach into the totes, discovering their new wardrobes. Kathy says to Laura "Maybe this is the new way to dressing, from here on out. They're treating us like children being taught a new way of living. Some of the girls are more willing to deal with this than others. We don't know when, but in time we all will begin to just blend into our new lifestyles. We'll start accepting it the best we can. Perhaps, the longer we're in it, the easier it will become to forget our pasts. We're gonna have to follow up in this new lifestyle." And the girls continue getting dressed.

Then the man opens a large cabinet with mirrors hanging inside the doors. It's full of little shelves which are loaded down with all kinds of makeup. Every color of eyeliner and lipstick. And every shade of powder.

"Okay girl's. It's time to get dolled up. Come on. Let's work on those faces. Get yourselves extra pretty. Come on, now. We don't have much time." Then he starts singling them out, "You two. You need to change tops. You. You know those don't match. Okay now, that looks good on you. And hey, can you smile little bit." Then announcing to all of them, "All of y'all. You need to practice smiling. Even if it's fake. I don't give a fuck. I see some of you smiling. I need to see a smile on all of y'all, now." He stood back, impressed, "Now, that's looking better. Let's get some makeup on, girls. Of course I mean, Ladies."

"Get them mops brushed, ladies. Each one of y'all. Gets the other one's hair. Come on. We got to make it fast." The girls work on their hair with brushes and hairspray. They powder their faces and gloss their lips with lipstick. Then they doll up their eyes, using the brightest of eyeliners. Kathy looks around the room thinking to herself. "It's like we woke up in a new world. I can't believe I actually have a pleasant smile on my face. At least for now. It reminds me of dressing up to go to prom. Both my body and mind are excited for this group thing that we're all in together.

Then, another man walks in the room. On that the girls hadn't seen yet. He is dressed up to the gills in a tuxedo, ready for a formal dance. He turns and looks at the girls. He is very pleased at the results. Kathy thought he didn't even look like he was one of them.

While the well-dressed man walks through the room, he looks at each of us. "Very nice. Very, very nice. You look lovely. Very beautiful. This is a very beautiful set of girls. We will find pleasant homes for each of you. I guarantee, you will be treated like ladies. And if you're not, you can come live with me. I have a huge house with a nice large swimming pool. I assure you that you will love it there. Okay ladies. You ready? It's Showtime. Put on your prettiest smile. How many you of you know how to walk sexy? Can you walk sexy, for me? Walk across the floor like this. Did y'all see that, now that is a sexy walk. Let me show you again how to walk sexy."

He puts his hands on his hips, putting one foot in front of the other and swinging his shoulders back and forth just a little bit, twisting his hips like he's trying to keep a ball up between them. When he leaves the room, some of the girls can't help but to laugh. They are already forgetting where there are.

The man turns to them and says, "I know, all y'all have watched fashion shows, at one time or another on TV. Remember how those girls walked? You must do the best walk you can do. You're gonna need to do it. The better the walk, the better the job. The better the job, the better your future. That's how it works, Ladies, for anybody in this life. Remember that as your walking in front of them. Twist your hips. Stop and turn. And don't forget to smile. Maybe, nod your head a little bit. Let them see that you're happy to be doing what you're doing.

"When the bidding starts, you need to walk around the floor's outer edge. And look into the booths where the gentlemen are sitting. Make sure that you smile a lot. And it won't hurt to wink your eye at some of them.

"Some of you may see a gentleman you feel attracted to. If he should ask you to stop and turn around, do so very gracefully. Turn your palms up, like this. Keep your arms downward, but out. Swing your hips to the right, and to the left. Just like this. Make a complete turn, just once. No more than that. Understand? Now, a show of hands. Who of you, believe you can so this? Good. I can see you're all together on this. Great. I am proud of all of you today. Don't be nervous. Remember, the highest bidders are the best jobs. You girls ready?"

One of the girls lets out a chuckle and giggles. "Hell yeah. Let's do this. I'm ready."

The guy watching over the girls remove the belts from around their waists. Then he drops them with the chain over in the corner of the room, like he was discarding it.

"Line up. Everybody. Line up, behind me." Then the other guy, the one that the girls seemed to forget had raped them, was down at the far end. He walks them in a straight line out of that room and into another room across the way. When the man opens the door, all that the girls can see are pretty red drapes, hanging down all around the room.

Kathy says to Angelique, "I can't even see the walls. And look up there," pointing to the five spotlights on the ceiling that are shining straight down into the booths.

After the girls entered the room, a man locked the door behind them. "Line up near the wall, behind the drapes."

Kathy can see a man sitting there, from between the drapes. He's all dressed up in a very expensive suit. In front of him is a counter draped by a black cloth, which flows over onto to the floor. A candle sits in the middle. And glass of water. Next to that was a small box, covered in buttons which were lit up different colors.

"Maybe that's how they bid." Getting curious, Kathy reaches out her hand and pulls back the drape just a little bit more. She sees a man with headphones on. "Maybe that's how he hears the auctioneer. This way, everything is very private."

The man with the tuxedo comes back to us. Pointing at the first girl he says, "Walk with me. He reaches down and lifts her hand gracefully. Then he stops and waits for her to look into his eyes. He gives her a pleasant smile and gestures with his head, "Walk with me." Then he leads her past the curtains and into the room. He escorts her around the room, like a prom date.

Meanwhile in another part of the building, Frank knocks on a door "Hey George. I didn't expect to find you here. Yeah, they called me in. Their other accountant, he took off sick. I've helped them out with accounting before.

"Do you mind if I sit in and listen as the auction starts? They've got some really fine looking girls here tonight and some really flamboyant bidders. This here, should be a real money-night. Especially if two of them bidders get into a bidding war against each other. One'll see a girl that reminds him of one he had years ago. He'll want some more of that. Maybe another one thinks that same girl is someone special. That's why the price goes so high. They just keep bidding. She's only one girl and she only gets to go home with the one who's willing to pay the most for her. There're some real top-name bidders here tonight." He looks down on George's desk. "Hey, look at that list. You see? Some of these here are from Canada and Colombia. And look. These guys are from Finland. And here. France and Germany. You know, those countries have some the biggest brothels and many of them like to change them out every so often. Keep it fresh for their clientele.

"These bidders from different countries each have different opinions about the girls. Different tastes. Different opinions of what a woman should look like. Some of them like a different variety. They may be looking for a certain type of girl. Or perhaps their clientele's looking for a foreigner. Maybe somebody in Germany wants only Chinese women. They've all got reasons for their preferences. And they definitely got the money. If they're smart enough to make the money, they're smart enough to make a good decision with that money.

"George. What ya gotta do is, make sure he gets supplied up with plenty of girls. Every two weeks. He's got a lot of people out there looking in the world. They're always calling him with their findings. Then they give him an approximate shipment date, when the girls will be here."

Then his friend George says, "Sit down Frank. Looks like the bidding is fixin to get started. See that guy out there, in the tuxedo. That one's a charmer. Watch. He's going to escort these girls around the room slowly, showing them off. But he's so smooth, it's almost like he's dancing with them. Me? I think he's the one that brings in the money. Without him, the girls would be nothing. They'd just be another pound of meat.

"See? He starts with the first girl there. And look, the bid is already starting to go up. He's got Canada bidding. And there. France bidding right behind him. See? He gets up when the first bidder signals and he stops, just for a second. See? He turns the girl around and then stands back, as if to look at her. Like she belongs to the first bidder.

"Now he's moving over to the next bidder. This guy's from Finland. Now, watch how our charmer lifts her hand up, high above her head, so as to spin her around gracefully like at a royal ball. Watch. He spins her really slow. Dancing. Oh, and see how the girls eat all this up? Right out of the palm of his hand. They just love it. Now he holds her there for just a moment. And tells her to smile. Watch what he does now. D'you see that? He started unbuttoning her shirt. He shows just enough cleavage. You know, part of the bidding is about the titties.

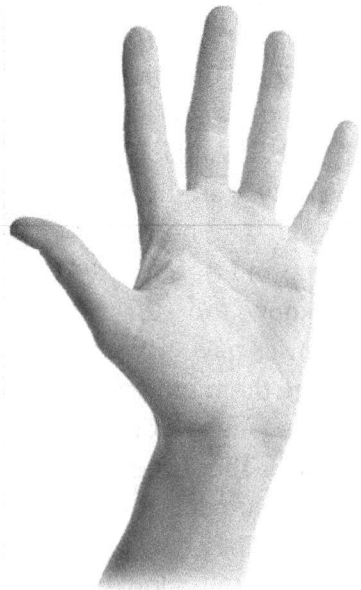

"Now you can see how he's moving around to the second booth. Those guys are from Canada. Did you notice when he spun her around that the bidding started going up? He walks her to the next booth. That's Columbia. Okay. See how the bidder reaches out for her hand? She has to reach over and hold his hand, even if just for a second or two. Some of our bidders think they can get a good feeling about the girl by holding her hand. It's like, they can read a girl better. He may even ask the girl a question or two. You know, to check out their personality a little bit.

"Now our guy is walking her over to the next booth. Let me look at my lists here. Let's see who that is. Yep. That's France. Notice how he asks her to lean in. He wants to look at her face up close. Now, walking her over to Germany, he spins her around.

"As she meets the last bidder our guy here takes her to the middle of the room. There she stands as the bidding finishes. After the suits complete their bidding, she'll be walked over to that door over there and put into a room where she'll wait until her bidder is ready to pick her up. Okay, see? She's going into the middle of the room. Right now, it's a close one between Columbia and Canada. Who's gonna get her? Looks like the bidding's done. Canada, for $15,000. Let me get that written down. Man, she is one of the prettiest ones I've seen in a long time. They will easily make their money back.

Chapter 17

"Alright now. Here comes the next one. Man, she's got some long legs and I like her hair. Guess I've always been partial to redheads. And man, look at those grapefruit-sized titties too. Mmm, all dolled in pink lingerie. Looks good under those spotlights. I bet she'll bring in some good money. And I like her auburn hair.

"Alright, let's listen. The bidding is starting and it's going to go up fast. Okay now, Canada's dropped out. It's just between Finland, Germany, and France. Okay, the bidding is still going up. It's up to $3000. Well, there goes Finland. Okay, it's $4000. $5050. $5050 and holding. Holding... Oh look, one final bid, 'Sold to Germany for $10,000.' Damn, I really thought she would bring in more than that. Didn't you?

"Oh, here comes the next one. I like the string bikini she's got on. Wait. He's gonna spin her around again. D'you see that? Her pussy is just bulging out there. Those bikini bottoms look like an ice-cream cone top. I'll bet she's a hot one. If she's not now, she's gonna be soon. Ok. Now the bidding's started. $2050. $3050. Alright, so far it's just Canada bidding. Wait. Columbia. And there it is. France. $4050. Going once. Going twice. $9000! Wow! $9000 for France. Going once. Going twice. Sold to France for $9000. I need to write that down.

"Ok, here comes the next one. Watch them come in from the dark of the room. Like, all the sudden it's just a magic act. Like, poof. Here's a girl. Can you see them here under the first spotlight? Then they just appear over there. It's magic. From dark to light.

"Anyhow, I like that aqua-blue see-through teddy. Does she's got on one of those bloomers? I can't tell. Now he's spinning her. Yep. That's what it is. Bloomers. I like the ruffles when they're hanging off their ass like that.

"Here it goes. The bidding's starting. $2000. $3000. Ok now. It's between France, Finland, and Columbia. We've got $4000. Now, France just dropped out. Ok, it's $5000. $5000 going once. Going twice. $8000. Going once. Going twice. Sold, to Columbia for $8000. Yeah, he got his money's worth. And he'll have all that money earned back in no time."

George asks Frank, "Well, what kind of guarantee does he have that once the auction is over the girls won't run off and leave the country?"

With a chuckle he says, "The bidder holds the girl's passport, and those girls can't leave without their passports. If they get picked up in another country without a passport they will go to jail."

"Okay. Two more, George. Here she comes. Oh, that ruby-red see-through lingerie top. Mmm, with G-string see-through bottoms. Yeah, I like how that pink fuzzy stuff runs along the sides of that G string. Oh yeah, d'you see that? When he turned her, that pink fuzzy stuff went right up her ass too.

"Ok. The bidding's started at $1500. $2000. $4000. Alright. It looks like the bidding is between Finland, Canada, and Germany. $7500. Going once. Going twice. Sold to Finland for $7500.

"Here comes the next one. Uh huh, that's cute. I like that. Looks like a cleaning lady. Black and white lingerie. The bidding is starting at $1500. $2500. Now, the bidding is between France, Columbia and Canada. We've got $3000. $4500. Looks like France has dropped out. $5700. Whoa, $12000! Going once. Going twice. Sold to Columbia for $12000. There it is. And he's definitely going to get his money's worth. Won't take him but a month.

"Just one more left for the evening. Where's she at? They must be having a hard time getting that girl to come out. I bet if they're gonna stick her with that stun gun. Then, she'll move that skinny ass of her's on out here. D'you see that They had to push her out. You can tell she's scared. Must not'd swallowed that pill that they offered. I've seen this happen before. That girl. She needs some more conditioning. Yeah, just some more conditioning. She'll be okay after that.

"The bidding starts at $1200. $2000. It's between Germany, Finland, and France. $2500. $3000. Okay, Germany's backing off. It's $9000, going once. Going twice. That's it. Sold to Finland for just $9000.

"Wasn't that fun Frank? I always hate to see it end. Sometimes, I get us a lot more girls at these auctions. Only the strong ones even make it this far. And yeah, a lot of them try to run off. Of course, that's when something terrible happens to them and they end up in the meat market."

Kathy was talking to Susan, "and after they walked me around that room with the lights, I noticed a small green light, over near the door. That door leads out of the room. One of the men came over, got me by the arm and led me out of room; through that very door where the green light was blinking. He walked me down the hallway and I noticed several doors. He unlocked one of the rooms and pushed me in. I didn't know what was going happen me. Seemed like minutes turned into hours. I could hear the keys jingling as the door was unlocking. When it opened, I was so glad to see that it was you, Susan."

The door opens and a man hands them some clothes. He then introduces himself, "Alexander. Now, get dressed and walk with me." Eagerly, Kathy and Susan get dressed and walk down the long hallway, to find a big metal door at its end. Alexander unlocks the door and the girls step outside. "Look, Susan. A van," pointing behind the building. As they get in, they are surprised to find six other girls.

Kathy had assumed Susan, Alexander and herself would be traveling alone. Alexander did not bother to explain the conditions to them, nor should he have to.

Quite a few miles down the gravel road, Alexander asked Kathy in a business-like fashion, "Okay, so you brought your passport along, right?"

Kathy nods her head, "Yes. The man, back at the building, handed them to us.' Kathy digs the passport out of her purse and holds it up.

"Great," Alexander said. "Let me have it. I'll hold onto it for your protection."

Kathy hands the passport over to Alexander, who then leans over to speak to the middle-aged man driving the Van.

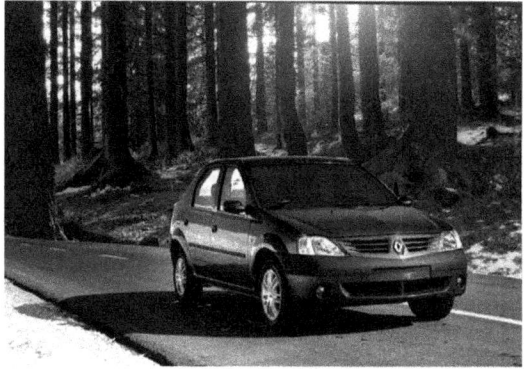

The man's eyes stayed fixed on Kathy in his rearview mirror, while they had their short discussion. The driver hands Alexander a roll of money.

Being that she was uncomfortable with the man's glare at her, Kathy turns her attention to one of the other girls in the far back. "Wait. Is that? She's that runaway. She's been missing for at least five or six years. She's aged a bit. I speculate none of them look like they've yet reached eighteen."

One of the girls lean over to Kathy with anxiety in her voice. "Do you know where we're going?"

"Susan and I were talking earlier. Alexander found me a job, working in a restaurant in France, as a matter of fact," Kathy replied

"Oh? That's what he told us that too."

Then one of the new girls said. "But I'm curious. Do any of you even know exactly where in France we're supposed to be going?"

Before Kathy can answer, the man whom Alexander presented as "the guide" promptly spoke up. "Listen up. We will to be changing vehicles in a few moments." Then proceeded with instructions. "Look up ahead. See those two vehicles? They are waiting for us. I will assign each of you to one of those two cars. Don't be troubled. It doesn't matter which car you end up in since we're all going to the same location.

We pull next to the two cars. Alexander gets out first. He picks up his suitcase from in the van and leads the way out to the door of the car. Kathy follows. As she and the other girls slide out of the backseat, Alexander assigns a vehicle to each of them. Alexander points to Kathy, who then slides right in, next to a girl she hadn't yet met.

The driver starts the car and follows the lead car out onto the blacktop. The two cars caravan for several hours. Kathy doesn't speak a word. She just keeps thinking, "Maybe this will turn out okay. Ya know; if they got us all jobs working in a restaurant, right?

Then Kathy passes the time, thinking about her mom. Then, in a panic, "Who cares if I can't afford all the things I want for my family? What kind of future would that be, without an education or at least a good job?" The rumbling of the car wheels sound like they're going to fall off.

Eventually they come to a stop at an airport. The men escort the girls in, Kathy right in line behind them. She stays with the group, knowing they had guns trained on them from behind. She was too frightened to try anything.

Just like the girl had told her earlier the check their didn't think anything was suspicious about these men handing her the girls' passports. They got onto the plane without a hitch. A fourteen hour flight later and they were in Hungary. They were herded outside where a new set of cars were waiting. Quickly they got in, the men making sure that they didn't pull anything funny.

The cars approach the border between Hungary and Romania and the two cars came to a sudden stop. It might've been close to midnight. Though the moon is bright, the full cloud coverage makes it hard to see. Kathy looks out the car window and sees drops of rain as it begins to fall. "Ugh. It seems we're in the middle of nowhere. Just some trees. A few bushes and those big rocks." Ten or fifteen minutes later they quietly wait. Parked on the side of the road.

Then a pair of headlights approach, slowly from the other direction as they headed down this pothole infested road. The car stops directly on the other side of the road from where the two cars are parked. The driver gets out and hurries his way over to the first car. The driver lets his window down and talks to Alexander for a brief moment. Then, he returns to the car that Kathy sits in and opens the trunk and then the back doors.

One of the men goes over the car, "Grab the bags that some of the girls brought. They're in the trunk." With a very commanding voice he says, ordering us, "You're changing cars for the next few miles of your trip."

Kathy moves to her newly assigned seat in the next car over and she peeps out the window. Across the road, she sees Alexander, sitting in the backseat of one of the cars the girls just got out of.

Kathy's senses a first whiff of trouble, "This sure is a lot of effort for somebody to go through to help us with a job. And why isn't Alexander coming along with us?" Kathy rolls her window down and waves her arms, trying to get Alexander attention. "He didn't see me."

Then she yells out, "Alexander!" Yet he gave not even a flinch or a look back.

She turns her head back around as the cars pursue on down the road, winding along the steep mountainsides. She keeps her attention dead ahead. Soon the two vehicles are passing a sign, "Romania"

"We must be at the border."

The two cars drive for several hours, after they've crossed into Romania. They continue down a dirt road, loaded with potholes. Then, the road gets very narrow as it turns into two paths; until the headlights are shining on some kind of building. Then the driver quickly yanks the steering wheel as he pulls up very close to an old country house.

Kathy turns her head to look out the car window, curious where she's at. She notices a valley and lights from a small village in the distance. "I wonder where we are. I have no idea. I wish I could ask, but do I have the right? Or would I be punished?"

The drivers bark out their orders and the girls move quickly and quietly into the house. The man ushers the girls into the house. They enter into a very dimly lit room. The six girls huddle together in the room. To their surprise, the man pulls close the door and locks it between himself and them.

Kathy turns around to notice three very young Romanian girls, sitting on a dirty stained couch, which is nestled over in one corner of the room. The lamp next to them reveals their lingerie. The girls fearfully stand up as the door swings opens. But then the door is pulled close again.

As they hear the click of the lock, they disappointedly slide back down onto to the heavily stained couch. Kathy turns to one of the girls and asks, "Can you tell me where we are at?"

"We're somewhere in Romania," replied a brown-eyed girl. She's a true beauty, but with such sadness on her face.

"How long have you been here?" Kathy is eager for any information. Any at all.

"Oh," said the brown eye girl, "I'd say, probably about two weeks. Maybe longer. To be truthful, it's hard to keep up. But it sure does seem longer than two weeks!" The girl exclaimed to Kathy.

Kathy turns back to the girls and asks, "Can anyone explain why we're here? What's going on?"

Chapter 18

The Romanian girl replies "I was told they're having some difficulty trying to get our tourist vistas." That's the only answer anyone offered to Kathy about their captivity.

A man brings them simple small meals, a couple times each day. They ask if they can go to the bathroom or walk outside around the house for some fresh air, but the man replied, "No. There's a big pot over in the corner. Use that for your bathroom." The man won't let them go outside. Nor would he allow them to step outside the room. Not at all.

"Why are we still here? Why are you keeping us in this room?" Kathy yells this out loud every time the man opens the door with their meal trays.

The man at first ignores her, but eventually gets tired of it. "You need to shut the fuck up!" he yells back as he sits down on the couch.

After seven days of confinement, a well-dressed man opens the door of the room. He is followed by a gangster-looking man.

"I have good news for you ladies," the well-dressed man says with a cheerful voice. "We have finally completed your travel vistas. So now you can continue your journey to Moldova! From there we're putting y'all on a touring bus that will take you to Poland. Your new jobs await you there. I have guaranteed apartments for each of you, so hang in there. You will begin saving money very soon after you get there."

The cheerful statement lifted the spirits of all the girls for the first time since getting to the house. Then the gangster looking man led the girls outside to an old farm house. As Kathy makes her way out the door, she sees two white vans, parked with their doors wide open.

Eagerly, the girls step up into the van to find their seats. "Such a relief after having been in that rat hole of a room for so many weeks." Kathy smiles at the other girls and for once actually thinks things will turn out okay.

They begin to venture up and over the mountains, winding around with the blacktop road. As the day continues the van hugs close to the narrow mountainsides as they cut across through the rugged country. They were going slow enough to avoid any opportunities for a treacherous accident. By the time late evening approaches, the van has ventured off the main highway and into the thicket, covered with trees and bushes.

The gangster looking man orders all the girls to get out of the van. The well-dressed man then says, "I could not contain a vista from Moldova, so the travel plans need to be altered...just little." He holds his hand out, his forefinger and thumb arched and almost touching one another. "But everything will still work out like planned. Girls. I got vistas for you to work in Poland. We were unsuccessful getting your travel visas to enter Ukraine."

Then he adds, "I will need for you to carefully sneak across border in the dark. Very quiet."

The girls complain in a very hoarse voice, "This is not what we agreed on."

Then the well-dressed man abruptly cuts them off, "I'm very
sorry for the inconvenience. Once you start working this day will
pass. This is the only way we can get you to where the tour bus is
at. It will take you to Poland." Then he added, "There are cars
waiting there for you. Just on the other side, at the Polish border.
The cars will blink their head lights four times, every three
minutes."

Then he warns with a concerned face and a frantic voice,
"Now, listen. If you're captured going across the border you girls
will be put into prison and they will throw away the key. Maybe for
years. Do you understand? Trust me. I have seen this before."
Then he lowers his worrying voice, "You don't want to be put in a
Ukraine prison."

The van drives down a narrow little path. Down a steep
incline and towards an opening in the woods. The sun sets in the
far west and darkness is soon upon them as they wait until they see
the lights flashing. The light filters through the trees from a good
distance.

"There, see? That's the car." the well-dressed man says as
he points his finger in
toward the
headlights. "Go, right
now, run until you
reach that ridge.
Right there where
those cars are parked;
but don't stop. Not
even for a second."

The girls step out of the car. It's as dark as black sackcloth. They can't even see their feet in front of them. They march across the rough terrain which is full of sharp rocks and covered with thorny vines. With fear threatening to take over they overlook the scratches, bumps and scars they get while crossing the treacherous ground while trying to not get caught; not wanting to go to prison for a very long time.

They continue crossing, sometimes stopping and stooping down real low, looking for the headlights. Then they see one blinking and they stand up, scurrying off toward the lights. They climb the last little hill to get to the car. Then someone realizes she only has one shoe. Her clothes are torn to the point of being rags and what isn't torn is scratched and bleeding.

Finally. They feel secure because they are in Poland. They walk toward the cars. The drivers continue to blink their lights.

After a couple minutes they are surrounding the cars, grabbing for door handles and eagerly climbing inside for safety because they were afraid that snakes and varmints would eat them alive on their midnight journey to safety. Then, faster than a mother bird feeding her young, they pack themselves into the two cars like two cans of sardines.

When the last car door closes the driver cranks up the motors and they make their way up the side of the mountain. They're traveling the treacherous curving road which eventually leads them to the other side of the mountain. The girls look out the front windshield, watching anything the headlights beam on. The car turns down another side road, still working its way around the mountain and onto the last little path.

As the sun was rising up, the girls could see to their surprise a little stone house nestled away amongst the trees and bushes. It would've made a perfect hideout for gangsters back in the early 1900s. The cars come to a complete halt and the doors of both vehicles open. The driver orders the girls to go inside the house, "It will be safer for you."

They enter the house filling up the little front room. Then the man orders them, "Sit up against the wall. Rest." He looks down at their shredded and torn clothes, their bruised and bleeding legs. Some of the girls just go ahead and kick off their shoes they are wearing. The girls look at one another. They can see the exhaustion in each other's faces.

All of the sudden the door opens and a slender, well-built blonde with a pretty smile on her lips walks through the doorway. She begins talking to the girls, giving them words of comfort. She has a perfect German accent. Then the woman turns, looks back out the door and talks to another woman bringing soapy water, towels, and rags so the girls can cleanup. The woman starts to turn to the girls, but then turns back, "Oh, and also, please bring something to clean their cuts and bruises."

Kathy and the other girls sit there. They took turns giving themselves sponge baths. The water had to be changed a couple of times, during which the lady tells them, "We need to be in groups of four. That's four to a bed." Then she tells the girls how their room is fixed up. "When you get through bathing you need to go out this room around the corner to the stairs and then follow them up to the top floor. Go on straight to bed. You need your rest for tomorrow. Get plenty of sleep," she urged them calmly.

When the girls finish bathing they ease themselves on up the stairs, just as the lady directed them to do. Soon, they fall off into a deep sleep.

Come noontime, they were still snoring away. The German lady and her female helpers wake the girls up with coffee and buttered Danish bread which was gently placed on the side. By this point they were famished. They hadn't eaten in days, they were constantly on the go.

The girls get into their second and third helpings. "Mmm, hot cinnamon butter rolls. And I'm gonna have at least two big cups of coffee." Kathy and her roommates fill their bellies until they're full.

The German lady walks out of the room and the girls go back to their room to lay down. They need to try to get some rest, but they are all so excited.

The girls stay up and share their stories, all they'd been through, with each other. About all the places they'd been. The Romanian girl, the one with the deep blue eyes who met Kathy at their last stop, was a roommate. One of the other girls traveled here from Turkey. She told her of her adventures from Iraq.

Kathy soon realizes that all the girls here were promised a job in Poland. For the first time since this had all happened to her Kathy felt safe...at least safer than she had been before. While not exactly her ideal situation, it was much better than what she had heard from the other girls. At least they weren't being beaten or forced to have sex with anyone.

Then the door swings open. It's the pretty lady with the German accent. "Okay girls, I need you to perform for me."

The girls stood there, looking at her like she was crazy. "What is she up to?" shrugged Laura.

Then the woman says, "These are your investors. They have put out a lot of money and a lot of effort to get you here. Before you go downstairs, you need to pull off your shirts. Everybody!"

At first Kathy thinks she has misunderstood the German accent. "Maybe she was trying to say something else, other than shirts." Kathy stands up, off the bed and turns towards the woman, "I beg your pardon, Ma'am, but I don't understand. What would you like us to do?"

Doing all she could to stay calm, the German lady repeats her order, "Take your shirts off. Down to your waist. C'mon. Let me see your breasts." She said it so casually as if to say it's time to go to school. Or, clean up your room.

Kathy, highly concerned, "You must be kidding me. I'm not used to just pulling my shirt off in front of a bunch of strange men."

The German lady turns back around to look at the girls, "Don't worry. Everything's all right. This is all part of checking you out for your employment at the restaurant. The business owner has sent these men to make sure that you are healthy."

The Lady can see the confusion as it comes across the girls' faces, so she adds, "In the past, some of the girls would become damaged on their trip here, which can imagine, creates a problem. This is just reassurance."

Kathy thinks out loud, "What's it going to hurt. They're just looking to make sure we don't have any diseases, right?"

"Right." Says the German lady. "This is right!" Kathy and the girls decide to go along with it.

The German lady turns back around saying, "Okay. Let's go. Drop your shirts onto the bed." The girls walk down the steps completely topless. Kathy can't help but to notice most of the girls breasts are bouncing as they walk down the steps. Soon, as they reach the bottom, the German lady motions to come over and lineup in front of the double doors. Like she was putting on a pageant. The girls can hear her holler out, "Okay. Okay, we're ready." She pushed the doors open to the front room and I notice about twelve well-dressed men sitting around the four walls.

We make it to the room. The German lady places us where she wants us to stand. Then she says, in broken language, "One at time. Say your name. Now, turn round slowly. All way round. Each every one of you. One at time."

Kathy turns and notices all the men staring at her and the other girls with full attention and sincerity on their faces while they make up their minds.

After the girls do a good job and have completed playing in their charade the German lady touches them on the shoulder and says, "Turn. One more time, slowly. Now, go back upstairs to bedroom." She then goes to the next girl and repeats the same thing until the last of them are out of the room.

After all of the girls make it upstairs they lay back down, trying to get some more rest. They nestle down in their beds and begin to doze off real good. The German lady darts back into the room, pointing. Pointing and saying very curtly, "You and you. Gather your things up. You two leaving with your new boss. Hurry. Go fast. He waiting."

The two girls gather what little bit they have and jam it into a brown, paper sack, like it was their overnight suitcase. Kathy and the other girl give their best wishes to their two leaving roommates. This was the first moment since their trip began that they've felt something so solid for each other.

"Good luck. Hope your job works out good for you,"

Kathy and the other girl scamper down the stairway, where a slender man with jet black hair is waiting for them. He says with his halting, German accent, "You, come with me. You work for me, now."

The man then walks them out through the front of the house to a suburban that's waiting for them. The driver was already in the front. The two girls are asked to get into the back and to put on their seatbelts. They drive for what appears to be hours until they get to a road sign with Rzeszow on it.

Kathy kept thinking, "We're gonna get to our new apartment soon. And we'll start our new job in the morning." They begin to make their way to the other side of the hill, to another house. "This might be our new apartment."

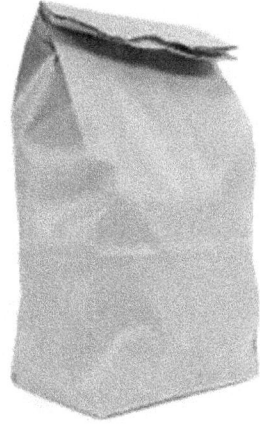

Chapter 19

Then their boss in the front seat turns and says, "Get out. Get out and go in." They all make their way into the house. The two girls become very confused and it's written all over their faces.

The new boss turns to the girls and says in his broken German language, "You. Wait here for me. I'll be back. One minute." They sit down, waiting for him to return.

A half hour had passes by when the front door opens. It's our boss. He walks in. And behind him are two well-dressed men.

"They look like maybe salesmen. That's what I'm thinking." Kathy really doesn't have a clue what's going on at this point, their boss hadn't taken the time to tell them anything yet.

The men eye the girls as though they are fashion models. You can tell the men are very excited by how they are walking, back and forth around us. Kathy is more confused now than ever. The two men begin to talk amongst themselves, in what sounds like Russian. Then it seems the two men came to a decision.

Their boss says, "Okay you work now!" Then in a sharper tone of voice, "I said, do. What? What do you mean, why work now? You cost me much money. It's time to pay. You. Go give good sex to these men. Now! You work."

The girls take several steps back, their eyes and jaws wide. They are both shocked. "This is not a restaurant job," says Kathy in a strong voice. "No way. I'm not doing that. You have the wrong idea. We're here to work. In a restaurant." Kathy was feeling desperate, "We will work really hard for you, at the restaurant. This here, this is not our idea of work."

Kathy then turns to look at the man they call their boss. She can see on his face that he has no patience for negotiation. She sees him reaching inside the pocket of his jacket, like he was going to give her a business card and Kathy begins to think she's got this worked out. He's pulling out something flat. She can't tell what it is, until he has pulled it all the way out. He goes to turn it and the light glints off the blade making Kathy's heart flutter. Her knees begin to get weaken. She thinks she's going to fall. Then with the speed of a cobra he reaches over and grabs her by the hair, pulling her back to him. He reaches over her shoulder with the shiny blade and presses it to her throat. The boss says shaking with anger, "You show these men a good time or I cut your throat."

Then Kathy says with tears in her eyes, "Okay, okay. Just calm down. We will go." Her voice shakes badly, nearly about to crack. She's too scared to fight back, not with that knife right there threatening to dig into her skin.

He goes to turn her loose, but then the two other men grabs us each by the arm and walks them each into different bedrooms. Then they are told to get undressed. "Get undressed or I'll call the boss." As the girls begin to get undressed, the two men begin to undress themselves as well.

Kathy is so scared. She doesn't know what's going to happen. The man reaches up and grabs Kathy, pushing her down onto the bed. She tries to tell him no but he slaps her hard. And then he slaps her hard again. "I can feel my lip. It's beginning to bleed. Or, I don't know. It might've been my nose bleeding."

He reaches down and pushes Kathy's legs up toward her chest. Then he begins fondling her down at her crotch. After a few minutes of playtime he has sex with her for an hour. He forces her to sit on top of him, as he lays flat on his back. At times Kathy felt like it was going up in her stomach. She isn't enjoying this. It's hurting.

Then the door flies open and the boss says, "That's enough. You're through. Leave." The man pushes me off of his body and gets dressed. As he leaves, the door is closed and locked.

A half hour passes and the door flies open. It is the boss. He says, "You. Go work, now." Then a man walks around him and into the bedroom. Then the door closes again. This goes on throughout the day and throughout most of the night.

Later on the girls are finally allowed to rest, locked up in a room together with just a mattress and as usual, a pee bucket in the corner. As they lay on the bed together Kathy turns to Angelique, "I'm guessing we've seen over twenty four men each on the first day."

After about a month or so passes, Kathy thinks she and the other girl might never get out of there. At least not alive. They continue having to serve twenty plus visitors a day.

One day Kathy is laying down on her bed, resting. The blonde headed German lady shows up once again. She walks over to the bed and leans over to put her hand on Kathy's face and in a calm voice she says, "These men around here, they're just a bunch of pigs. Always wanting. Wanting to just wallow on something or somebody. But now it's time for you to just move on. Let's get you out of here."

Kathy stands up off the bed. The lady looks at her like she has lost a lot of weight. Like she looks different. Then she says, "Looks like you both could use a hot meal."

Kathy remembers that this woman has deceived her before, but what choice does she have. If she's offering an act of kindness Kathy figures she should just play it out and see what happens.

"I finally got your passport straightened out so that you can work in Poland. You can work there in the Café."

The girls grab up their clothes and walk out the front of the house. Kathy keeps looking around to see if I see the boss. You know. The man who says "You. Go work, now." But there's no sign of him at all.

"I wonder what happened to him. It's like he's disappeared."

After the girls get into her car they drive downtown and pulled into the parking lot of a Café.

"Come inside."

"She is gonna feed us. Maybe she'll also let us get something to drink." Kathy is almost overtaken with all this kindness. She believes everything is going to be okay. They all sit down in a booth at the Café and place their orders.

The German lady shows them their passports, "See? They have been stamped. You're now protected. If the police should ask you for your documents you tell them you will be leaving in two days."

After they've eaten and gotten something to drink the blonde lady turns back to the house. She then says, "You owe a little more money, then I will give you your passports. You should work it off in no time." Kathy feels like she's gonna pass out.

They make their way back to the house. With discouraging looks on their faces, they continue serving both the boss and the German lady while the German man continues to bring more and more clients. It seems to the girls like they are each doing thirty men a day. It is just a constantly steady flow. As much as Kathy doesn't like it, she's at least beginning to see them as paying customers. It's just like any other business.

A couple of more days pass. Kathy and the other girl got a visit from two husky Russian men. "We are here to get you and transport you. You need to gather your belongings and come with us, now."

As they walk out the door, they can see three other girls in the van. They drive off and ride for many miles and miles.

Hours upon hours have passed as they finally come to a small town. One of the Russian men says, "We're going to stop here for a little while. This is called a 'safe house'."

On the fourth day they leave the house and drive for a couple of hours. They turn onto a little bitty path going downhill. It loops around to the right and then back to the left around trees. It is the beginning of nightfall. It's hard for Kathy to tell where she is and she's sure that nobody will answer her if she were to ask.

All of the sudden, Kathy sees lights reflecting off of the water. The man steps out of the vehicle. Kathy squints her eyes, looking out the windshield. She can see a very big lake with lots of trees around it.

The driver pulls up closer to the lake, his headlights shining across it. They sit there for about twenty minutes or so. Kathy rolls down her window to get some fresh air and she hears a motor boat. She looks around to see where the boat is and can hear it getting closer. But she cannot see it. All of the sudden, it pulls onto the shore, directly in front of the headlights.

The driver tells the girls to get out. "Go to the boat. Go with the men."

Kathy opens the door to get out and asks one of the men in the front seat, "Will this boat be taking us to Poland?"

"No. First you go to Lithuania."

As she hears what he has said, Kathy almost passes out. She begins to wonder, "Will this ever end? Will I ever have a life for myself? I don't think it'll ever end."

The headlights are still shining on the boat. They begin walking toward it and notice a large man in the back near the motor. They all step on board and the man says something. It sounds like Russian. The girls are confused so they just sit there. Then he points and touches one of the girls on the shoulder and then points to the front of the boat. He is wanting her to push the boat back into the water. After they get the boat turned around and head out into the waters of the Baltic Sea he powers up the motor. Fast, like he is in a hurry to get there.

He decides to start up a conversation with the girls, but nobody seemed to want to talk to him. He is old and he is fat, with lots of whiskers on his face and he is wearing an old, greasy hat. Of course, some of the girls have had to pleasure worse looking ones than him.

Every once in a while one of the girls answers him, just enough to be polite. They don't want to share anything personal about themselves to him. He says some sexually flirtatious things to the girls. He must've thought he could make one of them hot for him.

Time passes and they continue across the water. The man tells them that there are some shark-like fish down there. "Don't put your hand over the side of the boat." The girls begin to see a cluster of lights up a head. A small town, maybe. "I hope that's our destination we're approaching. I haven't seen much of the town. Just the bedroom."

The boat driver tells them that we don't have much further to go. The girls are all looking out toward the lights, when all of the sudden the motor quit running. First thing that comes to Kathy's mind is that they had done run out of gas. And there are all those shark-like fish in the water. "It's dark and we have this greasy, fuzzy-headed, bald man in the boat with us. And why should he be any different from all the others?"

The boat has come to a complete stop. They were just floating there. The man bluntly says, "I'm going to pick one of you to screw. Boat rides aren't free, ya know. I wouldn't mind taking a turn at all of y'all, but I'll settle for just one. I'll tell you now, the one I pick out better not screw me over or I will drown each and every one of you. One at a time. Let them shark fish eat you up. I don't give a god damn."

"We're gonna start right here. Right now." They all look at each other, fear on all their faces.

One of the girls hollers out in a concerned voice, "I can't swim." They try to think of a way to get out of this and realize they have no options. The man pulls out his knife and starts tapping it on the side of the boat to let us know he's still waiting.

Kathy looks over the side of the boat and thinks of just jumping in and swimming. "It looks really deep. Maybe there are shark-like looking fish in the water. Maybe the man can out swim me. Or maybe he'll decide to start the motor and run me over with the motor blades." She was running out of options. "Being with him can't be any worse than the other ideas."

The man pokes fun at them for being scared and continues to tap his knife on the side of the boat. They know he's going to make his selection soon. Fear creeps into their faces, deeper and deeper as they begin clutching each other's hands, gathering closer to each other in a circle. They can feel him fixing to make up his mind. One by one they begin closing their eyes and begin squeezing each other's hands. The fear of what he may do starts crawling through from one side of their minds to the other. One of the girls begins to shake so bad. She begins to cry.

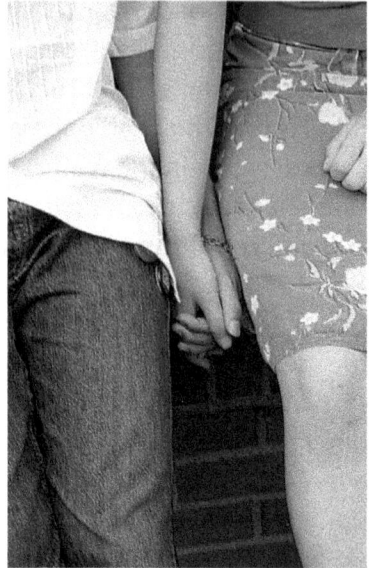

Then the big brute, tapping his knife on her shoulder with the side of his blade, says in a deep raspy voice, "You. Little blond headed girl. Come with me."

The girl doesn't fight it. She decides to go ahead and let him have his way with her. "No way I'm going to get out of this. That lesson has been proven, over and over again. Repeatedly."

"I told you to come here, Blondie. Don't make me turn this knife over. I'll use it on your throat. I bet your girlfriends'll even throw up."

All the other girls turn to the blond. "Don't be scared. Don't be ashamed. We've all been going through this for months now." They help her to stand up and turn around in the boat, so she wouldn't fall into the water. She'd get gobbled up by the shark fish for sure.

Slowly, she begins working her way to the back. To the driver. He reaches out with his burly hands and begins undressing both her and himself. The girls are scared the boat is gonna rock over because he is getting so overly excited.

He finally finishes violating her. They both get up. As they're getting dressed, he says, "You surprise me little girl. You put out real good. If you hadn't, I was ready to drown each and every one of your friends. Let the shark fish eat them," he began to chuckle. Then he cranks up the motor and heads to shore.

It looks like the little city is getting brighter. They continue to get closer and they can see a group of people up on the shore. At first, they could hardly make out the figures. But as they get closer, they begin to notice that these people are carrying big guns; and they're wearing uniforms, too. , Kathy can see Police written on the side of the car.

When Kathy turns to look, the boat driver does not look that surprised or alarmed over it. The first thing came to her mind, "We're going on up in one of them foreign prisons. We'll be there for the rest of our lives. Not having no way to get out." The driver drives the boat up onto the shore, making it steady. The girls get out, one at a time; while the police officer reaches over the boat to help steady them onto the shore. The officer escorts the girls up to the police car, putting some of them in one car and the other girls in another car. Then, they drive off. Kathy is so scared. "I'm going to prison now and I have no way of getting out.

"How ironic. After everything I went through to get a job, I'm gonna end up in prison." She thinks for a moment, "But maybe once we get to the police station, I'll be able to talk to the chief of police. Maybe he can help straighten this out."

Chapter 20

The girls continue driving through the small town and then back out the other side. I knew there was no police station that far out in the country. After short while and many miles to boot, the cars drive up upon a small house that was nestled in the woods by itself. By this point all of the girls were beyond nervous, questioning if these men were actually officers or not.

The police get out the front seat and open up the back door, walking all of the girls inside. No sooner than they got in the door, the officers start removing their uniforms, grabbing some of the girls by the arms, dragging them off into a private bedroom of their choice. They start raping the girls for several hours. Taking turns. Changing up partners. Laughing and cutting up. Sometimes they'd make Kathy do the same cop twice.

After about four hours the cops eventually left the house, leaving the girls in the care of a new pimp. Kathy just knew they wouldn't help them, her hope had been crushed long ago. She didn't care anymore.

"I consider myself very lucky to only have to spend a month here in the brothel in Shkodra. The Albanian pimps keep us girls moving on a treadmill. In fact, I once overheard them talking about how often they rotate the girls. I figured, they must have something worked out with the local police who visit the house a lot. Seems like they've paid off the cops for protection. I've seen the pimps bringing in a lot of girls, right through this avenue, just in the month we've been here."

One day, Kathy counted twenty-five individual encounters. There were always just too many men, each paying the house overseer to have sex with her. She very rarely ever got any real rest.

Kathy gets to know the other girls. Sometimes there will be up to eight girls at a time. As Kathy gets to know each of them, she finds out that some of them have been there for as long as six months. Some girls come and go. They might stay a couple months. "From what I can tell, those of you who've been here the longest, seems to be the most rebellious. The scars you carry are deeper."

"I remember, when the pimps came through on auction day to buy us girls, those girls who carried a good attitude sold for the best bidding. But all of the girls, even the ones who were a hundred percent submissive would get punched in the face by their pimp. Or he may even put a gun to her head. It's his job to keep reminding them, 'I am the boss.' They must do this to keep the girl from running off. Sometimes a pimp would get started on beating a girl and wouldn't quit until she was too bruised and cut-up to be used in a brothel. Then they would haul her off and no one would ever see her again. All we could do is hope that she was okay and hadn't end up in the meat market, to be sold for body parts."

"There was a girl here in the brothel. Her name was Connie. When she turned twenty two they considered her too old. Last I heard she had been sold to the Italians. One guy was snickering, '...and for some reason, the pimps tell me, they say they don't mind them older girls so much in Rome.'"

After a couple of weeks pass, the overseer tells Kathy, 'Get your things ready and come with me' So, Kathy walks out the door of the house to find there is a car waiting for her. Just idling. The driver is sitting in the front seat and Kathy is instructed to sit up front with him and go. The two of them take off. Kathy knows there really isn't any need for her to ask where they are going. She already knows she won't get an answer.

Kathy continues gazing out the door window, "It really is looking like a nice spring day. The leaves are beginning to bud on the trees. I like looking at the baby leaves as they sprout out. They're such a bright green. Maybe in another week or two they won't be so green. In fact, they'll never be such a bright green again; at least not until next spring. By autumn though, the leaves begin to die and turn brown, slowly falling to the ground. Waiting for Mother Nature to do her part, as the earth reclaims the leaf."

It becomes nightfall when suddenly the driver turns off the main highway and onto a small dirt path leading down a steep hill. He edges his car around through some trees and over some big rocks. Once the car quit bouncing Kathy was able to see a big lake right in front of them. The headlights beam off the water. The driver flashes his lights. That tells a story all its own, "I'm fixing to be picked up by a boat."

Kathy and the driver wait there for about a half hour. She continues to watch out over the lake, concerned about the boat, "Or what the boat driver may decide to do to me. But as much as I hate to admit it, this has become so routine to me. I speculate I know what's going to happen next."

Then, off in the distance, Kathy sees something coming to shore. The driver nudges her to get out. Kathy reaches to the floor to grab the sack of what clothes she has, what she has collected or obtained over the last several months. She reaches over, opens the door and steps out, then starts walking toward the boat. Kathy goes to step into the boat and notices that it is rubber with a motor on it. It is about five times the size of the one she was in the last time. If you're comparing boats, this one is the size of a bus.

Kathy finally gets in and finds a seat. She looks around at the others. There are a lot of people on board. Maybe close to thirty five or so. She sees a mother carrying a little bitty baby in her arms with a toddler sitting next to her knee. She gets settled in and the boat backs off from the shore. The driver gets the boat turned around and heads out to sea. Kathy can feel the wind beginning to pick up as it begins to sprinkle.

The boat continues on out into the sea. Kathy turns to look back. "There is no sight of land. The water should begin to get rougher soon as we continue on out to sea." The further out they go into the sea the rougher the weather and the waves. At times the wakes would pick the whole boat up into the air. Kathy is looking over the side, but she's really looking straight down a hill of water. The water brings them down again, like an elevator lowering them down into the water. It looks like they're in a room of water. Kathy is becoming very scared along with the other passengers. The children are screaming and crying. But when Kathy turns her head and looks at the driver he doesn't even look concerned. He just

throttles up on the motor as if he thinks he can out run the wave. He knows he'll make it to land in no time. But all the people begin leaning over the sides of the boat, throwing up.

After a little while passes, Kathy would lean over the boat again and throw up. She's turn back around and her face would get wet from the waves slapping it. As people are leaning over the boat to vomit, Kathy looks up to the front. She spots two goons, sitting there, trying to hold on. Then one of them turns and looks directly at Kathy. "Seems it's his job to keep an eye on me." she says as she wipes some bile off her lip. Then the children continue to scream and cry. "Is this ever going to end?"

One of the passengers reaches over and grabs Kathy on the shoulder. "Are you looking the lights of the Coast Guard? Here. Maybe you can get their attention with my flashlight."

Kathy nods her head, continuing to look around. The waves curl up the side of the boat, trying to take the boat crashing down with them, trying to flip them over. Swallowing them. The driver of the boat heads them upward toward the top of the water, making it harder for the wave to flip them over. As soon as he does, the driver faces another set of waves sent to challenge him.

The waves swiftly sideswipe the boat. He turns the boat straight into it to go over, "I have never seen waves this big before."

Kathy is more than just scared at this point, "I'm terrified of drowning. And what about the children? They too will drown." Then Kathy realizes, "It is in the middle of the night and there's not even a full moon out. I can't hardly see the waves in front of me, even with the spotlight from the boat." She shuts her eyes as tight as she can, trying to put this bad experience out of her mind.

Kathy holds her head down between her knees. Tears begin streaming out of her eyes, down to her cheeks. Kathy now finally admits the truth to herself, "I will never see my family again. This is the one thing in my life that I will not come out of."

She raises her head up. She can see some bright lights off in the distance. She turns and looks to one of the goons up front. "Is that France?"

"No. That's It-." He turns back and looks at Kathy as if to let her know that she doesn't have freedom, "Yes. I that's France."

Kathy didn't realize he was about to say Italy. Kathy gets excited and she begins saying, "France. France!"

The man turns back around, "Shut up. We're gonna put you out on the shore. There will be a driver there for you, if for any reason you get lost, there is a phone number and some money in that zip-lock bag I gave you earlier. You call that number. I will come get you."

"But, if for some reason..." he pulls his gun out from behind his back and puts it to Kathy's head, pulling back the hammer. "If for some reason you decide to run off, we have people on both sides of the water who will find you. Do you understand?"

Kathy nods her head with sincerity written all across her face, the intimidation tactic clearly effective against her.

He puts the gun back down and puts it behind him again, "Don't run off. We will hunt you down. There is no place for you to hide."

Kathy remembers when she got on the boat, one of the goons gave her something. She put it down in her bag with her clothes. Excited, she reaches down to see what it is. As she feels her hand around for it she pulls out a zip-lock bag. It has her passport and some money inside. Oh, and something scribbled on a piece of paper.

Now, perched in the hull of the raft, Kathy has a more pressing concern. The pilot has gotten the boat within twenty yards of the shore. While looking for the border patrol, he blurts out, "If he catches me bringing you across we are ALL going to prison. You'll always notice them by their spotlight. Be looking for it."

The man slows the motor down to an idle and continues to move in toward the cluster of lights, pouring out of the city. They get within three hundred feet of the shore. Then, all of the sudden, they see the spotlight and a voice echoing over the waters, "Hands in the air!"

The boat driver says, "Everybody! Get in the water. Swim down a little ways." As someone starts getting in the water, the boat driver continues, "If you don't get in the water, I'll put you in the water. Now, get out of my boat, quick. I got to go. I got to turn around." As he began to do that a couple of more girls jumped into the water. The boat driver walks to the front of the boat and pushes the lady and her baby over the side of the boat and into the water saying, "Get out!"

Kathy is hesitantly sliding down the side of the boat. She doesn't know how to swim. The boat is beginning to drift closer toward the shore, yet further from the cluster of lights. She still has one leg hanging over the side of the boat, scared to totally let go. Afraid she will drown. The boat driver walks over and grabs Kathy's leg, flinging it over the side. Kathy goes under.

Not sure what to do she starts paddling with her hands, while pushing off from the bottom with her feet. Kathy could feel the bottom, beneath the water. It felt sandy. As she tries walking toward the shore she can taste the salty water as it splashes into her mouth. When the boat driver turns the boat around making waves in the water Kathy can barely reach the bottom. From where she is standing the wave comes up and goes over the top of her head.

Chapter 21

The water goes up into her nose and mouth. Kathy's foot slips and she goes under again, for the fourth time. She goes under and tries to hold her breath. She pushes up with her feet as they reach the bottom, gasping for air as her head comes up out of the water. Kathy hears some shooting and then more shooting, but she can't see what they are firing at. Suddenly, she hears a large explosion. Flames light up the side of the bank. She sees a lot of trees and bushes. The sound of gunfire and screaming is absolutely deafening to ears. Then the light goes out. Kathy continues trying to make her way to the shore. She keeps slipping and falling. She is just so exhausted. She didn't get much sleep the night before. Then, unable to fight anymore, Kathy passes out.

The next morning Kathy can feel the warmth of the sun shining down on her face. It feels good. She doesn't want to move. At all. Kathy hadn't felt the sunlight shining on her like this for some time now. She hears a loud truck horn which brings her back to her senses. Kathy lifts her head and

moves her arms. She is still pretty exhausted. She didn't get much sleep. She is still exhausted from fighting the waters to stay alive last night. But she knows she needs to get up from where she is laying. She turns over and notices a big rock beneath her. There are bushes nestled on each side of it. Kathy stands up and reaches down in her pants, near her crotch. She moves her fingers around, "I found it." She pulls it out to look at it, just to make sure. "Yep. It's the zip-lock bag. Got my passport, a little bit of money, and a phone number scribbled paper. It's all there."

As Kathy is sitting there she contemplates, "If I call the number, what will happen? If I don't call the number what will happen." Kathy is beginning to feel hunger pains. She thinks about the money in the little zip-lock bag. "I could get something to eat. But if I do, will I have enough money to make a phone call?"

The more Kathy sits and thinks about it the more she realizes, "They've done everything they can think of to me. There's not much more that they can do to me, except to kill me. And honestly, after all that I've gone through, I'm not too worried about death anymore. Right now, I'm a little hungry and I want something to eat. Then I can think on it some more."

She stands there a little longer, giving an exhausted sigh, thoroughly enjoying the feeling of the breeze as it comes across her face. She can hear the birds in flight and she hears more birds in a tree behind her. "Sounds like they're making a nest." She looks out across the water and can't even see the other side. She turns her head to look down the bank and sees what's left of the rubber boat. There isn't very much washed up on the shore. The longer Kathy stands there near the water the more she enjoys the feeling of freedom; but she knows she has to be very careful.

Kathy looks out for the pimps and the police, too. "I gotta come up with a plan." Then she turns around and walks to the edge of the rock, finding a small trail. "Maybe it's an old fishing trail. I'm sure folks would come out to this rock to fish. I don't know. I'm hungry. I never did get a chance to eat last night before I left the house."

Kathy continues on down the trail until she sees the back of a building. She looks both ways, making sure nobody is driving down the road and walks around to the front. She sees it's a store. An old country store. The kind that's made out of old boards and an old tin roof. There's a bench out in front sitting right up under a window. Kathy walks over to the old screen doors. It has a big chrome handle which Kathy pulls, opening it right up. It makes a creaking sound. "This reminds me of when I was a little girl. Me and my grandmother would go to the store and get us a cold drink, and sometimes a cookie."

Kathy gets the screen door pulled far enough back to begin going up the steps. She is watching her feet, careful not to fall down. She is still exhausted and really weak. She notices the old board floor. It looks very old. Like old wood. As Kathy walks in she notices many old shelves. She begins walking down one of the aisles, "I wish I could find something cheap to buy. I don't have much money." Kathy turns and goes down another aisle. "There're some small loaves of bread on sale." She picks up a loaf and walks to the counter. There is a little old lady who meets her up at the counter. She was very pleasant and asks Kathy how her day is going.

"I've seen better." Then Kathy thinks to herself, "That lady might've thought I was a hobo. My clothes are all torn and I'm sure my hair is a mess. The old lady behind the counter rings her up. "That looks like one of those old cash registers. The kind you pull the handle on." Kathy reaches for her change as the lady hands it to her. "I know she handed back too much. She must be feeling sorry for me." Kathy offers a show of honesty as she offers the money back to the lady.

Kathy rushes out the door with her bread and eases around the corner of the building where she tears the wrapper off. "Remember. Eat slowly so you won't choke on the dry bread." As she is biting into the last piece of the bread she hears a screen door slamming shut. "I'm not sure if that's somebody going into the store or coming out." She looks around really quick to see if there is some place she can run to.

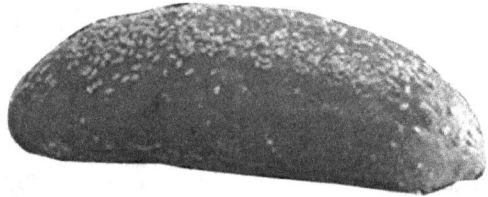

The older lady pokes her head around the side of the building. She is holding a glass in her hand and says, "Something to drink? Here. It's something to drink." Kathy turns to look at her more closely and looks deep into the old lady's eyes. She doesn't know if she can trust her, or not. "I have been deceived before. Over and over again. For a long time now."

The lady starts walking towards Kathy, offering the glass out to Kathy's reach. She has a kind smile on her face; and little wrinkles that go up around her eyes and ease out toward her ears. Her hair is almost totally gray and her dress looks kinda old, but is still in very good shape. "Oh come now, Sweetie, it's just some water. You must be thirsty?"

Kathy is beginning to feel safer now and she realizes that she is very thirsty. "All I've had to drink since last night was that salty seawater in my mouth."

Her trust has been broken time and time again. "It's still hard for me to let these people get close. At this point, I figured I should wrestle her to the ground. I've gotta take that chance." Kathy reaches out as far as she can, reaching to meeting her half way. As she reaches for the glass her fingers touch the top of the lady's hand. "She's very soft and her touch feels kind." Kathy pulls the glass toward her and takes a couple of steps closer to her. As Kathy begins drink, she starts crying.

The tears continue rolling down Kathy's cheeks and drip off onto the ground. Kathy hears the old lady saying, "Don't cry, baby. Don't cry. I may understand more than you know. Follow me around to the back. We'll go on through the back door and then you can wash your pretty little face."

Kathy feels the lady's hand on her arm as the lady begins to ease her around to the back of the building. When they make it around to the back steps, she pulls the little screen door open. Then she reaches up and turns the knob on an old door, pushing it open.

The lady steps back down, placing her hand under Kathy's arm, helping her up the steps. After they both make their way inside she closes the door behind them and begins looking around. "Wow, everything I see in here is old. It looks like it's the early nineteen hundreds." The lady reaches up to the middle room and pulls a string that turns on a light. Then she walks toward the sink and through a doorway. As Kathy followed her she notices an old bathtub.

"Would you rather just take you a bath? You look like you could use one and I bet you would feel better. I believe you're about my size."

Kathy turns back at her, puzzled.

"Don't worry, sweetie. You're safe here. It's okay. Go on. Go climb into the tub and get yourself all cleaned up. I'll fine you some pants. And a shirt. I believe the ones I used to wear in the garden will fit on you just fine."

This was the first time Kathy felt safe in a long while. When the lady returns with Kathy's clothes she knocks on the door of the bathroom and says, "Honey, I'm going sit your clothes just inside the door here. Oh, and there's towels in the cabinet, next to the bathtub."

Kathy says, "Thank you."

The woman turns to walk away from the door, "I feel pretty sure that that girl was part of some kind of human trafficking. I should probably call my nephew, Robert. My brother says that he is working within an underground task force that catches human traffickers."

The lady eases her way back up into the front part of the store. She walks over to the door and looks up front, just to make sure things are clear; that nobody followed her there. Feeling more at ease she turns around and walks back to the counter, picks up the phone receiver and begin dialing Robert's number.

"Oh great! It's starting to ring. God, I hope he's there. Hello? Hello, is this Robert?"

"Yes. Hi, Aunt Sharon. How you doing?"

"I believe I have something you'll be interested to hear. There's a young girl. She came into my store this morning. And she was showing some of the signs; you know, the ones that you told me to look for. And well, she's here now. Yes. She's in the back right now, taking herself a bath. I started thinking that you may want or need to talk to her. Maybe get some of the names or information you need from her."

"Aunt Sharon, keep visiting with her. But make sure you don't tell her I'm coming that way or she may get scared and take off. I should be there in about thirty five minutes. Okay? Alright, see you in a little bit. Bye-bye."

After hanging up with her nephew she makes her way back to the bathroom to check on Kathy. As she makes her way around the corner she gently steps up to the door, easing her ear over it. She can hear Kathy splashing around. "That poor thing. She probably hasn't had a bath in such a long time." Then she lightly taps on the door with her knuckle, "Are you okay in there, Sweetie? Oh, by the way, my name is Sharon. I didn't get your name.

"Yes, Ma'am. I'm fine. I was just a little dirtier than I thought, and my name is Kathy."

"Well Kathy, I have some homemade stew and some cornbread. Won't you come join me in a little while? We can eat? But take your time. Enjoy your bath. I'm not in no big hurry."

"Yes, ma'am. That sounds good. Give me just a few more minutes. Then I'll get dressed and I'll be ready."

Sharon quickly makes her way to the kitchen, turning on the fire under the stew and giving it another quick stir. "We don't want it to stick to the bottom now, do we?" Then she opens up the oven and cuts a big piece of cornbread. She lifts it out of the pan and puts it on a plate then hollers back, "Kathy! Kathy? Do you like butter on your cornbread, Kathy?"

"Yes, ma'am. Please. That sounds good. I'm getting dressed. I'll be there in just a minute."

When Sharon turns back around the soup has come to a boil. Then she turns the fire out underneath it. Sharon reaches over and gets her big spoon, then reaches up into the cabinet and grabs a bowl. "No. She doesn't want this little bowl. I think she's gonna be pretty hungry. We're gonna need one of these big bowls over here."

Sharon sets Kathy's bowl of stew down on the table and walks back over to put the cornbread in the microwave. "Just a little bit to melt the butter on top." Then she hears the pitter patter of little feet coming down the hallway. Turning around with a

motherly smile on her face she asks Kathy, "Are you hungry, honey? I've got your stew sitting right over there on the table for you. Oh, and the cornbread is in the microwave. It'll be ready soon."

When Sharon opens up the microwave, she can see Kathy out of the corner of her eye as she is coming through the doorway and into the kitchen. Sharon turns her head to greet her. "Go ahead, sweetie. Sit down. I'll bring you your cornbread." Then a thought runs through her mind, "I just can't help but to notice just how skinny she is. The clothes I handed her were a size small. Yet, they just hang off of her. Looks like I'm gonna need to find her a belt."

Kathy didn't waste any time sitting down and wrapping her fingers around the spoon. She began eating, scarfing it down as if she hadn't had any food in days. Kathy looks up at Sharon, "Aren't you going to eat?"

"No, sweetie. I done eaten earlier. You go ahead. Here's your cornbread. I went ahead and put just a little bit of butter on top for you. Okay? I hope you like melted butter on top. Do you won't tea to drink? I also have coke or water. Oh, and I have some milk."

"Milk will do fine, thank you. Mmm, and that's good cornbread. My aunt used to always make cornbread. Yep, every time I'd go visit her. Yeah, she liked to cook. I sure do miss her. She moved to Sweden."

Sharon notices Kathy peeping out toward the front counter. Sharon turns her head back around to Kathy and says, "I'm looking for my nephew, Robert. He's supposed to be bringing me a box of stuff." Just about that time, they hear the screen door slap against its frame. They look around the corner. And sure enough, it is Robert. Sharron makes her way around the counter and signals to him with her finger, pointing. "Let's go outside." And they make it down the steps.

Robert looks very concerned. "Where's she at?"

"She's in the kitchen eating a bowl of stew. She hasn't told me anything yet. But she fits the description. Everything you told me to look for. And she's real skinny, no more than a skeleton body. Dark rings around her eyes. I'm sure she hasn't slept in a week or two. Oh, and really hungry. How are you going to do this Robert?"

"Well, I could probably just go on into the kitchen. I'll let you introduce me and I'll tell her what I do for a living. Then we'll watch for a response. If she wants help she'll say something. If she don't, well then she'll cover up her story with a lie. In which case she'll end up going back to them. Some of these girls, well that's the only life they've ever known. It's the only life that they're comfortable with. As sad as it sounds, that's just the way life is. But if she wants to get out of it she'll open up to me. Come on. Let's go back inside. You can introduce me to her."

They make their way back up the steps and around the counter walking into the kitchen. Sharon notices Kathy's chair is empty. Sharon feels puzzled and frantic all at the same time. Trying to sound calm she hollers out for Kathy. "Kathy? Are you in here?"

"Yes, ma'am. I'm in the bathroom. Picking up my stuff."

Sharon walks back to the bathroom to check on Kathy, getting her to walk back to the kitchen. "Leave that alone, for now. I want you to come back to the kitchen with me and sit down. Would you like to have some coffee with me?"

"Yes, ma'am. That sounds good!"

Sharon stands there, looking down the hallway, waiting for Kathy to come around the corner from the bathroom. After a couple of minutes pass, Sharon sees her. As Kathy gets close to the kitchen door she sees Robert. Her face must've looked like it went on red alert because Sharon says, "It's okay, Kathy. This is my nephew. He's going to drink coffee with us, too.

When Kathy turns back into the kitchen she notices Robert getting a cup from the cabinet while Sharon makes her way over to the stove. "Kathy? Do you like cream and sugar? Or just straight up black?"

Kathy replies with a gentle but nervous smile on her lips. "Cream and sugar'll be fine. I like for my coffee to look kinda muddy."

Kathy asks Sharon, "Can I sit right here at the end of the table? I don't want to take the chair you usually sit in."

"That will be just fine. You sit right there. And here's your coffee sweetie. Imma let you put your own cream and sugar in, okay?"

Sharon pours herself a cup of coffee and walks over to the table to sit with Kathy. She takes a sip of her coffee and can see Robert was pouring his cup out of the corner of her eye. He turns around and grabs the back of the chair and pulls it out. Then, setting his coffee down on the table, he says, "Kathy. My name is Robert.

"I work for an underground organization. An elite task force. Our mission is to stop human trafficking. I belong to an organization called the GRP. We work side by side with government officials. Our task force tries to shut down traffic organizations. We mainly work underground, in secret. We have agents who play their way into an organization. Gaining trust, so as to find the traffic lords. Coming up with such information as addresses and contact information."

Scooting up closer to the table Robert crosses his arms and folds his hands together. Letting his chin rest upon them he gives Kathy a friendly, warm smile. "Now, Kathy. You may tell me that I'm wrong. But judging by your appearance and from what I see I believe that you just escaped a sex trafficking ring. My organization can help to relocate you and your family. If needed we can send you to a neutral country. We can keep you safe. But we need you to help us with some names and other information. It would be good if you can help us. Anything that may help lead us to arrest some of the sex trafficking lords. What do you say? I can guarantee you safety if are you willing to help me. Like I said, just help us with some names and information."

Kathy's face has a look of shock as she starts to stutter, "Oh yes. You're right. And Yes. I would like to help. Yes, I know a lot of names. But first, I must definitely have safety for my family." Her heart beats fast as she realizes she is finally through with her nightmare.

Summary

Kathy worked alongside with Robert in the GRP group for many years to come. She has since relocated to Sweden. She is there with her family and has been reunited with her daughter.

Since this time, Kathy has gotten married and has two more children. She has become a strong member of the GRP group. Working with them and other organizations as they try unite to put a stop to human trafficking.

Other books you might find interesting by Paul Cote.

A boy Named Jinx;
(From the gates of hell and, Rises up from the ash).   *Written By Paul (Jinx) Cote.*

The little rascals, Tom Sawyer, on steroid or high octane fuel, during the hippie years, About a young boy that finds his way through life, due to a corrupt, dysfunctional environment at Home, turns to living in the streets and learning a new way to survive.

The Book starts with signing into a mental Ward, during treatment multitudes of interesting stories will arouse from his pass, Then being released, and working hard to have a better life, and trying not to drag along as much baggage cause from the past.

The book holds 42 plus Blended stories, with psychology, dispense, action, drama, and romance;
Too many chapters to mention here check out the inside of the Book.
The names of certain individuals included in this book have been changed to protect their privacy.
Warning Comes with Strong language.

The adventures of Todd and Suzy;
Written By Paul Cote.

Enjoy a magical mystery tour of truth historical places as Todd and Suzy investigates the pass in a soon discovered Time Machine, take the journey with this brother and sister teenagers, go into the pass and feel the presence like being there with the ones that made history, even if you're not a history buff at the same time very educational, you will still find it exciting to travel with them.

Feel the passion and the presence of visits with some of; 1. The Wright Brothers. 2. Thomas Edison. 3. Albert Einstein. 4. Alexander Bell. 5. South End Grounds (baseball) in Boston. 6. Boston Fire. 7. Boston tea party. 8. Abraham Lincoln. 9. Amelia Earhart. 10. Florence Nightingale. 11. Dr. Martin Luther King, Jr. 12. Steamboat ride. Intended for the readers of age 8 and up to the adult kid.

Flat rock;

Written By Paul Cote.

The story is about an Indian spiritual world that comes back for revenge and trying to regain its people's land that died on the trail of tears. They find their selves nestled down in a Canyon next to a RV Park on the outskirts of a quiet Highway; they sacrifice on a blood red moon, the campers in order to satisfy the God of earth, and then from time to time having council meetings up in the spiritual world in the heavens, Have you been thinking about camping? Warning has horrified violent language.

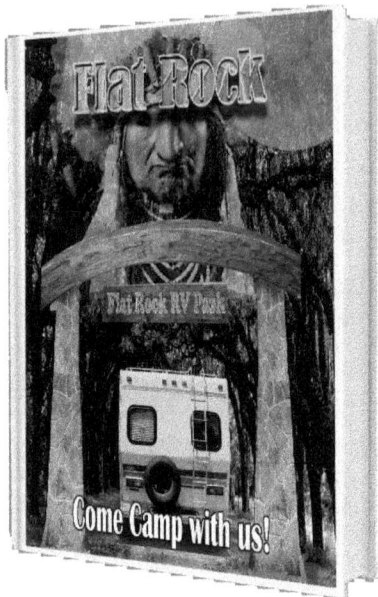

Lots of Suspense, Action, horror, some true history, the story is built up around the characters and their encounters of;

Chief's names;

Head Chief; Sitting-Eagle.

Which Doctor; Bear-Wolf.

Chief; flying-eagle, Chief; mad-Hatter, Chief; Sitting-by-cloud, Chief; painted-pony.

Warriors; Broken-arrow, Raging-bull, Screaming-heart, Thundercloud, Sunbeam, Storekeeper; black-bone.

Warning Comes with Strong language.

For Resale information or to ask about other Books Please Contact H. Paul Cote at
3348 Arkansas Rd. West Monroe La. 71291
Paulcotes@yahoo.com

www.ingramcontent.com/pod-product-compliance
Lightning Source LLC
Chambersburg PA
CBHW052129270326
41930CB00012B/2814